Emyl Jenkins' Guide to Buying and Collecting Early American Furniture

BOOKS BY EMYL JENKINS

Emyl Jenkins' Appraisal Book

EMYL JENKINS'
GUIDE TO
BUYING AND COLLECTING
EARLY AMERICAN
FURNITURE

EMYL JENKINS

with

Joe E. A. Wilkinson

CROWN PUBLISHERS, INC., NEW YORK

Published by Crown Publishers, Inc., 201 East 50th Street, New York, New York 10022. Member of the Crown Publishing Group.

CROWN is a trademark of Crown Publishers, Inc.

Manufactured in the United States of America

Library of Congress Cataloging-in-Publication Data

Jenkins, Emyl.
Emyl Jenkins' guide to buying and collecting early American furniture / by Emyl Jenkins with Joe E. A. Wilkinson.—1st ed.
p.   cm.
Includes bibliographical references (p.   ) and index.
1. Furniture—Expertising.   2. Furniture—Reproduction.   3. Furniture—Repairing.   I. Wilkinson, Joe E. A.   II. Title.
NK2240.J47   1991
749.213—dc20   90-2369
CIP

ISBN 0-517-57085-8

10   9   8   7   6   5   4   3   2   1

First Edition

To Janella Smyth,
who holds our hands and tolerates
our many anxiety attacks

CONTENTS

CONTENTS

FOREWORD

*A*nyone—museum employee, antiques dealer, auctioneer, or collector—who is familiar with the current market is very much aware of the problems involved in authenticating American antique furniture. The vast number of would-be collectors and some amateur dealers, many of whom have only the most rudimentary knowledge of the field, and the prominent position enjoyed by auction houses whose personnel respond to all criticism by pointing out that everything is sold "without warranty" and "as is" have led to a situation where the buyer must not only "beware" but also be knowledgeable.

There was a time, of course, when novice collectors could move gradually into the field, often under the tutelage of an experienced and ethical furniture dealer, buying a piece here, a piece there, usually at prices modest enough to assure that mistakes would not prove particularly costly.

Today, though, collectors are often given little time to acclimate themselves to a rapidly changing market. Clever auction promoters urge them to get in on the "action," while dealers unknown but a few years ago take out full-page advertisements in antiques and living publications to tout their wares, "guaranteed" to be better investments than gold, jewels, or the stock market (that other quicksand for the uninformed!).

Given the realities of the present antiques marketplace, it is important for every collector to learn as much as he or she can about furniture or any other item to be collected. Knowledge is the best defense against deception or against the honest mistakes that the many dealers new to the field are likely to make and then pass on to their customers.

Unfortunately, however, the world of antiques is a complex one and that of antique furniture particularly so. It is difficult for a commentator, no matter how sincere, to put down in one volume sufficient information to guide the novice through the pitfalls of fakes, reproductions, concealed restorations, and the myriad other problems facing today's collector.

In their book Emyl Jenkins and Joe Wilkinson have come as close as anyone is likely to in putting together a guidebook for those who are considering purchasing and collecting Early American furniture. Not only do they carefully analyze each individual eighteenth-century furniture style, but they also point out how each resembles and differs from those late nineteenth- and twentieth-century reproductions referred to as "Colonial Revival."

This discussion is accompanied by numerous examples of individual pieces, which are examined top to bottom in such a way as to provide a framework within which the individual can approach similar pieces in the marketplace. While there are never any guarantees against being fooled, and while all of us make mistakes, it seems likely that anyone following the step-by-step process set out by the authors will be well on the way to establishing the sort of expertise that will minimize errors. In the turbulent arena that is the present-day antiques world that is really all one can hope for!

WILLIAM C. KETCHUM, JR.

PREFACE

From a distance the tilt-top table had possibilities. But in the dim light of the antiques shop storeroom, I couldn't be sure. Approaching the table, I saw immediately that it recently had been refinished. The maple was pale, lifeless. There was no depth or warmth of patina that builds up with years of dust and dusting. There were no blemishes or evidence of loving use. But the table was still worth a closer examination.

Taking it out into the light of day, I began my inspection. No tools were needed—just common sense and an inquiring mind, plus knowing where to look and what to look for.

"The latch is old, but new to this table. The top and the pedestal were recently put together. The iron strap was put underneath the pedestal column to hide the new feet," I ticked off to my friend, who more than once has asked, "How do you know all that?" "Now let's see what the tag claims," I said, saving the worst news for last. *Eighteenth-century New England maple tilt-top table. $3,800.*

"Well, it is a maple tilt-top table," I conceded. "But only the top is eighteenth century. And it probably was put together in New England," I added. "But its price should be closer to $800 than to $3,800 and a collector wouldn't touch it."

How had I known? Simple. Objects do not lie and each point from the finish to the hardware held its own clues, told its own story. For example, around the latch there was the shadow of a different outline. If that latch had always been present, no other outline could have shown up. Releasing the latch and looking at the bottom of the tabletop, I had seen an impressed round mark. The top surface of the current pedestal was square. Squares do not leave round marks. These two parts had obviously been matched up, or married, when the original pedestal had been replaced. How could I tell the pedestal was the newer piece and not the top? The top showed signs of wear—underneath, not on top. You see, to make the piece look "right" it had had to be refinished so the mismatched top and pedestal would be the same color. Looking at the feet, I had not seen any signs of two hundred years of wear or the dovetail construction where the feet joined the center column. In fact, an oversized securing iron strap had been placed there to hide the incorrect, modern dowel construction.

No tools had been needed. No lab tests had been necessary. What was needed was just a thoughtful step-by-step analysis, the sort every collector should take the time to go through before spending $800 or $3,800 only to discover later that he or she has made a wrong purchase.

But the problem is how to remember all the fine points to look for when you're standing in front of a fabulous piece and have to make a decision in a heartbeat.

Joe Wilkinson and I have come up with a two-part format in this *Guide to Buying and Collecting Early American Furniture* to make your job easier.

Part One allows you to learn by reading at your leisure. Though you may forget much of the information you read, you will remember where you can find it. And much of what you read will come back to you when you need it. You will know to proceed cautiously when examining the object of your desire and not be carried away in a moment of passion.

The case studies in Part Two distinguish this book from many other sources and will make it possible for you to make the great buy or keep from being had. This section is designed as a working tool to have in front of you as you analyze, *step by step,* each major point before making your final judgment and deciding *yes, it is* or *no, it isn't* a period antique.

Carry this book with you if you can. Keep it on top of your current reading stack. Copy the case studies. Make note cards. Use whatever technique works best for you, but keep the case studies within easy reach. And don't be surprised when you see others using them. Even experts need reminders of where to look and what to look for when a great find—and money—is on the line.

PART ONE

How You Can Be the One Who Makes the Finds

ll true lovers of antiques live for that one great find: the wonderful antique sold for a mere fraction of its real value.

Everyone hears of such phenomenal finds as the Queen Anne Philadelphia lowboy purchased for $25 off the back porch of a tenement house or the museum-quality Rhode Island shield-back armchair sold as an English chair by a New York auction house for one-twentieth of its $75,000 value.

Whether the find is made in Biloxi, Mississippi, or New York City, an instant judgment has to be made: Is this *really* a fine American period piece? Or might it be a good reproduction, a fake, or a heavily restored or altered piece? A fortune can be made or lost by knowing the *right* answer on the spot.

For example, let's say you're browsing through the many shops in an antiques mall. You spy a mahogany piecrust tea table with relief-carved legs. The price is $1,500. Before you write your check let's see what the possibilities are that you're making a wise investment.

First, there's the chance that the table is a fine old reproduction, one dating from the late nineteenth or early twentieth century. Some excellent copies were made in those days. But $1,500? That's a substantial price for a reproduction—if it is one.

But what if it isn't? What if it really is an eighteenth-century American table in fine, unrestored condition? Fifteen hundred dollars is only a fraction of its value if the table is an American period piece.

Then there's another possibility. What if the table dates from the eighteenth century but is an English period piece or a restored American period piece? Then it's a good buy at $1,500, but of course it isn't the "steal" it would be if it were an American period piece in pristine condition.

You must decide. If only you knew what to look for!

Virtually every great find requires a split-second decision based on a quick, accurate assessment arrived at by on-the-spot analysis plus the awareness that such a find can be made anywhere at any time.

Why are so many finds overlooked? Because few antiques buyers are aware of how many fine pieces slip by unnoticed. How often have you heard an antiques dealer exclaim, "You just can't find a good buy in American period furniture anymore!" But the pickers and the astute buyers know. Believe us, finds can be made anywhere at any time.

Proof? Just a few months ago, when visiting a country antiques dealer, Joe and I heard those very same words. As the dealer was speaking, we spied a fine early-nineteenth-century neoclassical side chair.

"How much for the chair?" we asked.

"Oh, that? . . . A hundred dollars."

We bought the chair, sent it to auction, and an avid collector happily paid $1,600 for it.

The moral? Even seasoned dealers can lose the

These two pictures of the same chair illustrate the once-in-a-lifetime find. The family knew the chair was from Philadelphia and dated from the eighteenth century. But they had no idea its grungy old finish would be pure gold to the connoisseur. When the chair sold at Sotheby's, the catalog description clearly stated the specific condition of the chair in 1989. But an old repair to the crest rail and the stationary cushion, dropped in sometime in the nineteenth century, did not deter anyone from bidding. The sale price was $77,500 (plus the 10 percent buyer's premium). Who says there aren't any finds around these days? The secret is being able to identify the unmistakable marks of true American eighteenth-century craftsmanship and knowing which repairs affect value and to what extent. Photo above, courtesy of Sotheby's

awareness that such finds still can be made.

How can you become the buyer who makes the finds? Take a lesson from someone who spends his life distinguishing the real from the counterfeit, a U.S. Treasury agent. "I hardly ever study counterfeit currency," he admitted. "But I spend endless hours studying the real thing."

Just like the Treasury agent who can spot a counterfeit bill at a glance, the antiques collector can learn to spot the counterfeit antique by studying the genuine antique. The reproduction, the restored piece, or even the outright fake antique will be-

come obvious with the help of this book and the firsthand study of fine antiques.

There can be no substitute for hands-on experience with American period furniture. Now, through the use of our checklist, you, the potential buyer, will be able to cut through the myriad details that once were only mysteries or problems.

Perhaps you've been too embarrassed to ask a dealer, appraiser, or auctioneer the questions you really *need* answers to: What am I looking for? Where do I begin?

After giving a talk on furniture a few years ago I

noticed a young woman at the back of the group standing around the podium waiting to ask questions. It wasn't until the others had wandered off that she summoned the courage to approach me.

"Emyl," she began timidly, "I've always been afraid to ask anybody this question, but I don't think you'll make fun of me. For years I've noticed people at antiques shops and shows going up to a chest of drawers, opening the drawers, and running their hands under the drawer bottoms. Then they either smile or they frown. Now when I look at a chest of drawers I always open up the drawers and run my

No one claims that learning about antiques is easy. Many collectors have fine old reproductions in their homes that they bought as period antiques. The chair on the left is an American Queen Anne chair of the rural variety and dates from the 1730 to 1750 era. It is important for every collector to know that these chairs, and almost every other form of eighteenth-century American furniture, were being reproduced at the turn of the twentieth century, and often, as the illustration on the right proudly proclaims, "Made with the Colonial construction of wedges, by chair makers who have inherited the art from father to son." Ralph Erskine advertised his Troy, North Carolina, workshop's products in the national publication Arts and Decorations *in the 1910s. This particular chair cost $15 in 1913 and was delivered free anywhere in the United States.*

Shop of **RALPH ERSKINE**

Interesting Chairs

Made with the Colonial construction of wedges, by chair makers who have inherited the art from father to son

hands under the drawer bottom. Most of the time I smile. Would you please tell me what I'm smiling about?"

The lesson to be learned from this innocent question is that many people give the appearance of knowing all about antiques and even pronounce judgment on the authenticity, correctness, or quality of antiques without having the vaguest idea what they are even looking *for*—or *at*!

You may already know that the bottoms of drawers have telltale clues that reveal whether a piece is manufactured or handmade. But if you don't, now is your chance to learn. If you already know many hints and clues to identifying true American period antiques, reviewing these points and learning others will make you an even more astute collector.

Believe us, no one knows everything, and there are times when even the experts call other experts to talk things over and get another point of view. In fact, when we decided to write this book together and began sketching out the contents, one of us would bring in a point the other had overlooked or even forgotten about, and sometimes had never thought about before.

So whether you are a first-time buyer or an experienced collector ready to weed out your collection or upgrade, this book is designed for you. The simple step-by-step procedure for examining furniture outlined in the following pages is the tool that will turn both the puzzled neophyte and the seasoned buyer into knowledgeable experts.

2

THE OTHER SIDE OF THE STORY, OR HOW TO AVOID BEING TAKEN

*T*here are so many wonderful finds awaiting the astute, knowledgeable buyer that it's tempting just to tell you about those opportunities. Yet, as appraisers, we often find ourselves spending as much time being diplomats as being appraisers when we must tell our clients that the highboy they thought was an eighteenth-century piece was really made in the 1920s or that their 1800 corner cupboard has been glamorized by adding new butterfly-shaped shelves, string inlay, and ogee bracket feet.

If you've made mistakes in the past, don't despair. So have great collectors, knowledgeable curators, and first-rate dealers. Who hasn't heard about the "Brewster chair affair"—the story of how Armand LaMontagne spent two dollars and two months purposely creating a seventeenth-century-style chair and aging it? LaMontagne then watched his chair pass through various experts' hands until it was purchased by the Henry Ford Museum for $9,000 and pictured on the cover of the museum's collection brochure.

Or you may have read about the fake dower chest in the Winterthur collection. Or, if you're really up on the subject, you may have attended the exhibition "April Fool: Folk Art Fakes and Forgeries" at the well-known Hirschl and Adler Folk Gallery.

But these are the glamorous exposés. What about those pieces we see every day in antiques shops, at auctions, and in our clients' homes that simply are not what they are purported to be?

Many times we are called in by owners to authenticate their pieces. Often the owner wants to know if his chest can possibly be an eighteenth-century New England chest. (It probably will be.) Sometimes the question is whether all twelve chairs are true Philadelphia period chairs. (They probably won't be.) Another type of question we are frequently asked is, Is the piecrust, tilt-top table English or American? (It might be either one.)

But then there are the times when we must tell an unsuspecting owner that his piece, whether inherited or purchased, is not an American period antique piece but rather is:

• a fake or a fraud—made with the intention of deceiving the purchaser

• a true antique—but having changes, alterations, repairs, replacements, enhancements, additions, or even subtractions (shortened, parts removed, and so forth) sufficient to seriously affect the value of the piece

• an old reproduction—the honest piece never intended to deceive, but with sufficient age and family history (the owner's or someone else's) so the current owner mistakenly thinks the piece is 50, 100, or 150 years older than it really is.

Interestingly, of these three groups—(1) the piece designed to deceive, (2) the substantially restored or repaired piece, and (3) the old reproduction—it is the third group, the old reproduction, that currently has the greatest value in the marketplace and that will most likely continue to increase in value over the next few years.

Many faithful reproductions have a niche in today's market, particularly those turned out by high-quality furniture manufacturers who used fine materials and often incorporated handcrafted steps in making the pieces. Labeled pieces by such companies or workshops as Kittinger, Margolis, Charak, Wallace Nutting, Baker, Berkey & Gay, and others are being quickly grabbed up by collectors who want fine-quality pieces in eighteenth-century styles, but who cannot afford the more expensive true period antiques.

The famed, faked Brewster chair was built by Armand La-Montagne to intentionally deceive connoisseurs and curators. He succeeded. The chair was purchased by the Henry Ford Museum and used to adorn the cover of one of the museum's collection brochures before its true identity was uncovered.
Photo courtesy of the Henry Ford Museum

Though this mass-produced secretary from 1930 is forty years away from becoming a "legal" antique, and the serious student of antiques quickly recognizes that its top is incorrectly proportioned for it to be a faithful copy of an eighteenth-century secretary bookcase, it would still be quickly purchased if offered for sale in fine condition in the $1,000 to $2,000 range.

Governor Winthrop Secretary No. 1259

A beautiful example of the famous secretary desk so popular now. A large well designed desk with three large drawers, and with roomy bookshelves with attractively designed grille glass doors. Height, 75 inches; width, 38 inches; depth, 19 inches. Mahogany veneered. Average weight, crated, 250 pounds.

There are many true antiques that have been "improved" over the years. The owner of this now very glamorous eighteenth-century Virginia secretary bookcase told me herself of how she took the once simple piece to the local cabinetmaker and had him raise the cornice to accommodate a newly carved blind-fretwork frieze and add ogee bracket feet. The money he charged to enhance the secretary in the 1930s or 1940s is nothing compared to the thousands of dollars the owner was throwing away by having these changes made.

The larger case pieces, secretaries, breakfronts, and dining tables are usually the most expensive of the old reproductions. And why not? As the cost for a truly fine-quality *new* reproduction secretary bookcase exceeds $14,000, and an eighteenth-century American one exceeds $30,000, the good early-twentieth-century reproduction secretary becomes quite appealing at $1,000 to $3,000, while even finer ones soar from $3,000 to $5,000 and higher.

And old reproductions of those pieces everyone wants but that are no longer being made are bringing even more money, especially when turned out by quality-conscious companies. When a reproduc-

tion Queen Anne–style mahogany bonnet-top highboy by Margolis was auctioned at Clearing House Auction Galleries in Wethersfield, Connecticut, in mid-1989, it quickly surpassed its preauction estimate of $4,000 to $6,000 and sold for $10,900.

But even old reproductions can be confusing to the novice. Understanding how these nineteenth- and twentieth-century copies of eighteenth-century pieces evolved will help you more quickly distinguish between the fine-quality reproduction and the poorer-quality reproduction.

Most nineteenth-century copies of earlier eighteenth-century styles that you may *mistakenly* think are true period pieces were made during the

One of the fastest-moving markets in the antiques world to-day isn't for antiques at all, but rather for those extremely fine old reproductions of true period pieces. When this early-twentieth-century mahogany bonnet-top highboy, made by the Margolis Company of Hartford, Connecticut, sold at auction in 1989, it brought a surprising $10,900. Photo courtesy of Clearing House Auction Galleries Inc.

This rather faithful reproduction of an eighteenth-century Philadelphia armchair would give many potential buyers problems. There are differences that the expert would see, including some stylistic and some technical differences, but more people would be deceived than would question its authenticity. The chair, from the Rhode Island School of Design Museum of Art collection, was made between 1880 and 1883 by Sypher & Company, a New York City firm. Photo courtesy of Museum of Art, Rhode Island School of Design, Bequest of Commander William Davis Miller

WITH its rich simplicity, its quiet grace and its dignity, the Colonial always will hold a high place, if not the highest, in the regard of true admirers of the tasteful in furniture.

This stately Colonial Highboy of solid Mahogany is a fair example of the excellence in design, material, construction and finish which is characteristic of all our pieces.

$165 00
Width, 40 inches
Height, 89 inches

W. A. HATHAWAY COMPANY
62 West 45th St. New York
"Furniture of the Better Kind"

The life-style magazines of the 1910s contained untold numbers of advertisements for "Colonial" pieces. Some seventy or eighty years later, many of these are mistakenly thought to date from the eighteenth rather than the twentieth century.

DISTINCTIVE INTERPRETATIONS OF PERIOD DESIGNS

A Barnard and Simonds interpretation of an historic chair invariably results in a distinctively beautiful piece of furniture.

The cunning of Chippendale's art, which produced one of the most interesting and imaginative of all furniture styles, is skilfully reflected in the graceful design of the chairs illustrated.

In addition to an extensive variety of period pieces in authentic renderings, our line of fine seating furniture includes an unusual number of the popular English and American Windsor chairs.

BARNARD & SIMONDS COMPANY
ROCHESTER,   NEW YORK

Many twentieth-century designers used eighteenth-century styles as the basis for their designs but adapted or interpreted these styles to fit twentieth-century ideas of fashion.

DUNCAN & DUNCAN, Inc.
1830 Spruce Street, Philadelphia, Pa.
Reproductions & Antiques

GALLATIN SOFA
Length: 84 inches

It fairly breathes the
spirit of the old South

Made of selected mahogany
Carving sharp and true to period

See our Exhibit at
THE KAPOCK HOUSE EXHIBITION
Philadelphia

By the 1920s antiques were so popular that even Empire pieces from barely a hundred years earlier were being reproduced. This ad not only appeals to the nostalgia of pre–Civil War days, it also promises that the sofa will have sharp carving and be true to the period.

When these two pieces were given hands-on examination it became obvious that both had undergone alterations before their appearance in the 1902 book Furniture of the Olden Time.

1870–1930 era. Before that time the new Victorian fashions of the 1840s through the 1860s dominated. But by the later 1870s, a reaction to the elaborateness of the Victorian style, combined with the interest in American colonial days inspired by the centennial celebration, led to a revival of eighteenth-century styles. The result was the mass-manufacturing of Queen Anne, Chippendale, Hepplewhite, and early Sheraton reproductions.

The very best pieces made during this time were *faithful* copies of eighteenth-century designs like the Sypher chair illustrated here.

The natural aging of these pieces over the past 70 to 110 years, as well as the materials used and, in some cases, even construction techniques, can lead to confusion between the fine-quality, faithfully copied old reproduction and the true period antique.

A quick look at the life-style magazines of the 1910 era shows advertisement after advertisement of "faithful copies" of every imaginable form of furniture, even pieces from the Empire period. Alongside these are advertisements of "adaptive" pieces or later "interpretations" of early period designs. The Barnard & Simonds Company illustration from the December 1916 issue of *Good Furniture* is an example of these types of pieces. And then there were the furniture lines that were so obviously mass-produced by twentieth-century machines and tools that they would be immediately recognized as such. Chapter 4, "Don't Overlook the Obvious," expounds further on these reproductions as you learn the fine points that distinguish eighteenth-century pieces from later reproductions.

But early on let us caution you about assuming

that early-twentieth-century books on antiques are good and reliable sources of information. During this era, as Americans followed the collecting fad begun by Rockefeller, DuPont, and Ford, to name three illustrious collectors, a flood of books emerged. Many of the illustrations were of pieces that began life in the eighteenth century but that had already been tampered with, or "enhanced," by the 1910s and 1920s.

One such example created a particularly delicate situation for me. I was asked to appraise a collection that included several pieces that had descended in the family of Frances Clary Morse, author of *Furniture of the Olden Time*, an enormously successful book first published in 1902 and reprinted in 1903, 1905, 1908, 1910, and 1913. In 1917 a new edition came out with a new chapter and new illustrations, and twenty years later, in 1937, yet another new edition was issued, and other reprints followed.

Two of the pieces in the collection were prominently featured in *Furniture of the Olden Time,* one a Federal or Hepplewhite card table and the other a dressing table or lowboy. Careful inspection showed that the classical urn inlay on the center panel of the card table was a later addition, or enhancement, to the table. Furthermore, the lowboy top was an old replacement. How old was the top? When had the inlay been added? Sometime before 1902.

Our purpose is not to discourage you. We cite these illustrations to encourage you to read on, to learn, and to become the one who will make the true finds and not be taken in by a fake, altered piece, or reproduction.

Despite the H. C. Valentine Company's claim in their 1930 catalog that this chair is designed after a 1790s chair, no one today could confuse it with an eighteenth-century chair's design or construction.

3

BEFORE YOU BEGIN: THE PROPER NOMENCLATURE

ifteen years ago two lovely ladies came into the antiques shop where I was working. They were looking for a piece suitable for displaying several porcelain figurines.

"What you need is an upright vitrine," I told them, and, careful to use the correct terms for these French ornaments, I proceeded to point out two different types of vitrines in stock: an inlaid mahogany Hepplewhite-style vitrine and a Louis XVI–style vitrine with carved cartouche and bronze-doré sabots and chutes.

"My dear, what did you say you call these pieces?" one of the ladies asked, unimpressed with my attention to the decorative details.

"Vitrine," I repeated. "It's a term for glass display cases. Some are like coffee tables and have the glass on the top so you look down into the piece, but others are standing pieces, like cabinets, with glass doors and sides so you can look straight into the piece and see the objects."

The ladies looked suspiciously at one another and mumbled something about wanting to look around a little more. But as they left, I overheard one of them say, "Imagine calling a china cabinet a latrine, and she looked like such a nice young lady too!"

Our point is an important one. Before you can begin to look at furniture intelligently, you must know what to call specific pieces and their individual parts. Consequently, we start with a glossary of the terms you will find throughout this book. There is no reason to memorize these terms, but we do suggest that you familiarize yourself with them now. Then, when you come across a term in the text you do not know, you can take the time to check back before continuing.

JUST WHAT IS AN ANTIQUE?

Though most people use the same terms to distinguish specific pieces and parts of furniture, if you were to ask any group of individuals just what an antique is, you'd probably get a variety of definitions. For that reason, we give our definition of the term *antique* now so you will have no doubt as to what we mean.

THE LEGAL DEFINITION

When the U.S. Customs Service allows an item to enter the country duty free as an antique, they require that the piece be at least a hundred years old. This legal definition of an antique is a sliding gauge. The antique of 1991 would have to have been made in 1891 or earlier. More precisely (and absurdly), at 12:01, January 1, 1992, a piece made in 1892 becomes an instant antique, whereas two minutes be-

A piece of furniture made during the original time frame of the design is called a period antique. This c. 1770 Chippendale chair is correctly termed a period Chippendale chair. Photo courtesy of Craig and Tarlton

fore it was merely old. We will *not* use this legal definition in our book.

THE CONNOISSEUR'S DEFINITION

Many collectors use the term *antique* to refer to items made before 1830 or 1840, the era when mechanical tools and techniques replaced earlier, handcrafted processes. However, this is an arbitrary definition based on the premise that a handcrafted item is always superior to or better than a manufactured item. This simply is not true: A crudely constructed table made of inferior materials and

design is not necessarily superior to a manufactured table made of outstanding materials and design. Again, we will *not* use this definition of *antique* in our book.

PERIOD ANTIQUES AND LATER RENDERINGS

Rather, we *will* use two important terms that define the age of a piece by the originality of its design combined with the time it was made. These are terms all serious antiquers use, and you must know them. They are *period* and *style*, and they are used to distinguish the true antique from the later copy. These terms are so important that both Sotheby's and Christie's (and many other houses as well) carefully explain their use in the front of each auction catalog.

First, the definitions:

Period. The term used to denote that a piece was made during the original time frame of the design.

Style. The term used to denote that a piece is in the fashion or nature of an earlier period but made at a later time.

Now let's see how easy it is to use these words when you understand their application.

The Chippendale chair (named after the well-known English designer of furniture) illustrated here became fashionable in America around 1770, after being introduced in England about twenty years earlier. Chippendale chairs of this type are characterized by their shaped crest rails, pierced and carved back splats, splayed back legs, and carved cabriole front legs that often end on ball-and-claw feet. For approximately twenty years, or until about 1790, when the new Hepplewhite fashion became popular, American craftsmen turned out thousands of Chippendale chairs similar to this one. The chairs made during those years are correctly termed period Chippendale chairs. The word *period* implies that the chair (or table, lowboy, or whatever) was made at the original time of the fashion. The pieces made between 1755 and 1790 in

On the other hand, furniture made at a later time but in an earlier style should always have the word style *included in its description to distinguish it from a period piece. This chair, made around 1880, is therefore correctly termed a Chippendale-style chair.* Photo courtesy of Museum of Art, Rhode Island School of Design, Bequest of Commander William Davis Miller

this fashion are the true, unquestionable Chippendale pieces, which, by any definition, are antiques.

Over the next hundred years furniture designers were busy creating new fashions—Hepplewhite, Sheraton, Empire, and Victorian pieces. But in the 1870s Americans became fascinated with the furniture fashions of what they called America's Pilgrim, or Colonial, days. Designers then began to re-create pieces in the Chippendale (as well as Queen Anne, Hepplewhite, Sheraton, and Empire) fashion.

There were, however, many changes made by the designers and the makers of these later Chippendale chairs. To begin with, the 1870 pieces were often mass-produced with the help of power-driven tools in the furniture factories. (You will learn on the following pages how to distinguish between

handmade nails used in 1770 and machine-cut nails of the 1870s.) Hand-planed boards used in the mid-1700s were replaced by circular-sawed boards in the 1870s. (You'll learn how to make this distinction too.) Furthermore, many designers of the 1870s took nineteenth-century liberties with the 1770 designs. As a result, some of the 1870s chairs copied after the 1770 design have different type legs or different proportions from the 1770 Chippendale chairs. Or, in other words, one hundred plus years after the original Chippendale chair was made, other chairs were made in the Chippendale style, but with differences that had evolved in the interim.

Some people will call that 1870 Chippendale-style chair an antique because it is more than a hundred years old. We will not, because we are seeking the true, eighteenth-century Chippendale period piece. We will help you avoid being taken in by the 1870 chair, which is either masquerading as a 1770 chair (after all, the 1870 chair is now 120 years old itself!) or is being sold by an unknowledgeable person as a 1770 chair.

So from this point on, the word *antique* will refer only to those pieces that are of the period when the original design was created.

THE WHOLE IS THE SUM OF THE PARTS

In the following chapters you will learn where to look and what to look for, before spending your money, in order to determine whether the piece you are considering is a true period antique or not. To know where to look and be able to converse intelligently with other experts—you see, you'll soon be an expert yourself—you first must know what to call what you're talking about.

The rest of this chapter is devoted to a glossary and labeled illustrations to familiarize you with the proper nomenclature for various furniture forms. Construction terms (*mortise* and *tenon joint,* for example) are not included here as these are discussed and illustrated in the chapters that cover these points in depth.

Also, remember that names of parts are interchangeable. Thus, when you see a part or element named on one form—for example, the apron on a chest of drawers—realize that the term is applicable to the same element on a lowboy or secretary. We do not rename every part in every illustration.

So here, for you to study now and refer to later, are a brief glossary and illustrations of several major furniture forms and the names of their individual exterior parts. Following the illustrations are line drawings of many of the motifs and decorations found on American furniture. Dictionaries devoted entirely to furniture and decorative arts terminology are listed in the Bibliography.

GLOSSARY OF TERMS

Astragal. A simple convex molding, used to divide panels.

Apron. The last horizontal strip running between the legs of either a chair or case piece and above the void of space; interchangeable with *Skirt*.

Banding. A strip or strips of veneer that outline a shape; usually found around drawers or a case frame and in contrasting color or pattern.

Bead. A strip of wood used as a molding. See *Astragal*.

Birdcage. The support beneath the top of a table attached to a pedestal with freestanding columns at the four corners.

Blockfront. A shape composed of three sections with the center recessed or outset.

Bowfront. A convex curved front.

Breakfront. A large piece of furniture, usually a three-bay piece with the center section outset.

Canopy. Technically the fabric or cover above a bed; used generically, the term denotes the frame for the fabric as well.

Canted corner. See *Chamfer*.

Carcass. The frame or body of a piece of furniture.

Case piece. A piece of furniture intended to store or hold items; for example, cupboards, chests, secretaries, and desks. Beds, chairs, sofas, and tables (even with drawers) are not case pieces.

Chamfer. The cut-off or beveled edge of a corner.

Cornice. The projecting straight or horizontal portion at the top of secretaries, breakfronts, wardrobes, etc.

Crest rail. The horizontal top rail of seating furniture; it can be in many shapes (straight, bow, scrolled, etc.).

Cross rail. The horizontal rail of a chair back beneath the crest rail, often carved or shaped.

Drop. A hanging ornament used for decoration and usually found in American period pieces on lowboys. Also called *pendant*.

Drop front. A writing surface hinged to a desk front; interchangeable with *Fall front* and *Slant top*.

Drop-in seat. A separate chair seat that can be removed from the seat frame; interchangeable with *Slip seat*. The opposite of *Tight seat*.

Drop leaf. A hinged section of a table that can be raised and supported by various means (a swinging leg, for example). Many types of tables—Pembroke, gate-leg, dining, and so forth—are generically called drop-leaf tables when this section is present.

Fall front. See *Drop front*.

Finial. An upward-projecting ornament found at the corner or along the top of any piece of furniture. The opposite of a drop or pendant. Finials exist in countless designs, shapes, and forms.

Frieze. The horizontal section just below the cornice or molding of a case piece or just below the tabletop of a table or chest.

Gallery. A raised rim that surrounds the top of a surface, usually either entirely or on three sides. It may be reticulated, open (as a gallery rail), or solid.

Glazed. Filled with sheets of glass; used to describe glass doors in cupboards. The opposite of panel doors.

Inlay. A pattern or design usually of wood, but possibly of other material (mother-of-pearl, brass, and so on), that is "laid into" the surrounding wood.

Molding (also **moulding**). A strip of wood that is usually functional as well as decorative and is most often found along the edge, frame, top, or bottom of another element or part of furniture.

Panel. A solid area of wood that is separate from the surrounding piece; most often a panel door or headboard panel.

Pedestal. A support for a top, or the support for a

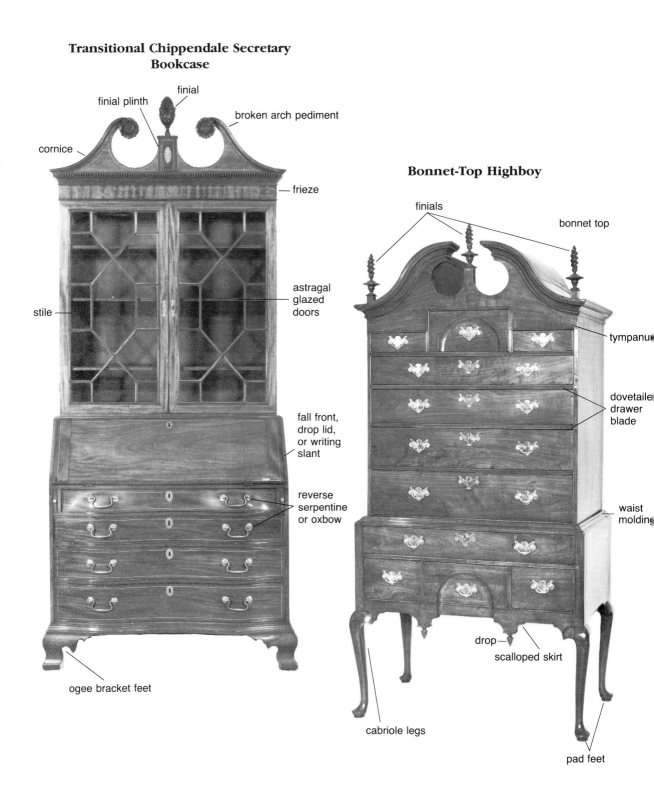

Transitional Chippendale Secretary Bookcase

finial

finial plinth

broken arch pediment

cornice

frieze

astragal glazed doors

stile

fall front, drop lid, or writing slant

reverse serpentine or oxbow

ogee bracket feet

Bonnet-Top Highboy

finials

bonnet top

tympanu[m]

dovetaile[d] drawer blade

waist moldin[g]

drop

scalloped skirt

cabriole legs

pad feet

Chippendale Chest of Drawers

molded top

escutcheon

bail brasses

quarter column

base molding

ogee feet

Federal Bow-Front Chest of Drawers

crossbanded edge

bow front

ring pulls

inlay band

splay feet

scalloped skirt or apron

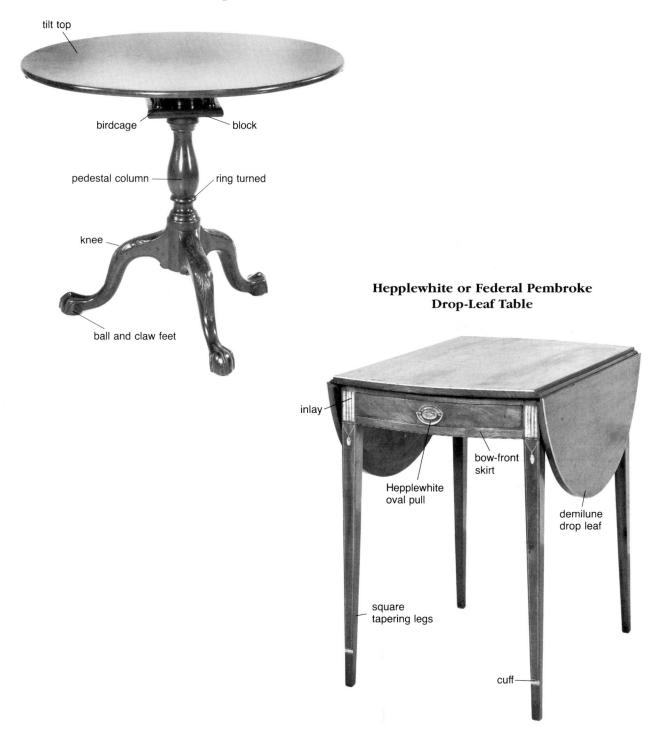

Queen Anne Tilt-Top Table

tilt top

birdcage

block

pedestal column

ring turned

knee

ball and claw feet

Hepplewhite or Federal Pembroke Drop-Leaf Table

inlay

Hepplewhite oval pull

bow-front skirt

demilune drop leaf

square tapering legs

cuff

Hepplewhite or Federal Shield-Back Armchair

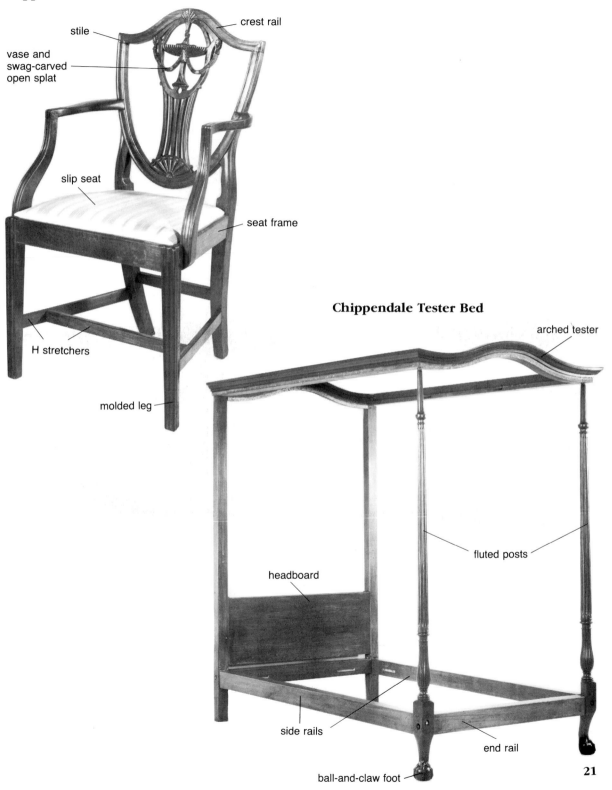

stile

crest rail

vase and
swag-carved
open splat

slip seat

seat frame

H stretchers

molded leg

Chippendale Tester Bed

arched tester

fluted posts

headboard

side rails

end rail

ball-and-claw foot

Furniture Decorative Motifs

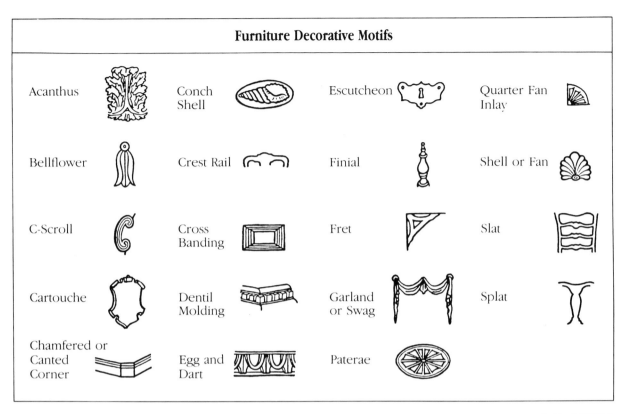

Furniture Feet and Legs
(These can be clues to identifying styles.)

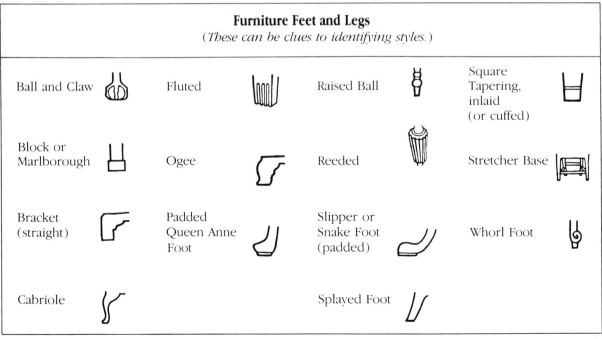

column. Because columns are an element between the top and the base of tables, in furniture, pedestal can refer to either the column or the base. For clarity it is best to use the term in conjunction with the specific part, for example, pedestal column or pedestal base.

Pediment. A geometric architectural feature that tops a case piece. Most pediments are further described by their shape and decoration, for example, scroll pediment, broken arch pediment, etc.

Pilaster. An ornamental half column applied to the surface of a piece of furniture.

Rail. A horizontal bar of wood that runs between two ends. See *Slats*.

Seat rail. The horizontal wood that runs between the four legs and is shaped or plain that supports the seat.

Serpentine. A curving shape, convex at the center, concave at the ends.

Skirt. See *Apron*.

Slant top. See *Drop front*.

Slats. The horizontal strips of wood between uprights; used when speaking of ladder-back chairs or bed parts.

Slip seat. A removable seat. See *Drop-in seat*. The opposite of *Tight seat*.

Splat. The vertical strip at the back of a chair between the *Crest rail* and the back seat rail.

Stiles. The vertical elements that frame the rest of the piece.

Stretchers. Horizontal connecting strips running in a variety of ways between the legs (most often of chairs and tables) that strengthen the weight-bearing elements but can also be decorative.

Surround. A feature that forms a border to a design.

Tester. The frame above a bed from which fabric (the *Canopy*) is hung.

Tight seat. A stationary (nonremovable) seat attached to the outside of the seat frame rather than fitting inside the frame.

4

DON'T OVERLOOK THE OBVIOUS

Remember the young woman in chapter 1 who wanted to know about the drawer bottoms? Though many pieces will give themselves away on the first look by their outward appearance, we've seen overeager antiquers begin on the inside or underneath without taking the time to look first at the outside. True, the insides and underneaths, even the backsides, are important, but often the front will tell you ... Is it or isn't it? If you make your first examination a long, thoughtful observation, you may not need to look further.

BEGIN ON THE OUTSIDE

The five areas to concentrate on during a frontal inspection are

> style
> proportions, dimensions, and size
> materials
> color
> the price tag!

STYLE

Without question, knowing the correct characteristics of each American eighteenth-century and early-nineteenth-century style is your best safeguard nineteenth-century style is your best safeguard against making a blatant mistake. The literature on American eighteenth-century furniture is vast. We would fail dismally were we to try to cover all its

Style: **Queen Anne**
Age: **1720–1760**
**Primary woods most frequently used: walnut
and mahogany, some cherry and maple,
especially in chairs and case pieces made in
rural areas**

Queen Anne pieces are most quickly identified by their lovely curves and graceful lines. The scrolling lines of chair crest rails and pediments on secretaries are two such examples. Often Queen Anne pieces terminate on cabriole legs that curve gracefully outward and the aprons or skirts on chests, tables, and other case pieces are often scrolled and scalloped.

These pieces were featured in furniture catalogs some fifty or more years ago. Most people would realize the chest with attached mirror is not a period antique by casually glancing at its outside. The build-up of fifty years of wear, wax, and patina on the outside of the Chippendale-style highboy might lead you to think it dates from the eighteenth century. But the interior construction quickly gives away its twentieth-century origin.

variations, nuances, and subtleties here. Rather, the paragraphs that follow are devoted to the four eighteenth-century styles you will encounter most frequently on your great American treasure hunt: Queen Anne, Chippendale, Hepplewhite, and Sheraton.

STYLE: Chippendale
AGE: 1755–1790
Primary woods most frequently used:
mahogany, walnut, and cherry

Chippendale furniture is usually distinguished from Queen Anne furniture by its straighter, bolder lines and heavier feeling. The delicate scrolls and curves give way to straighter and stronger lines. Compare the Chippendale pieces illustrated with the Queen Anne pieces and you'll see the differences immediately. Though you may find curving lines on Chippendale pieces, you see that they are framed by a more geometric perspective than the freer, looser curves of the Queen Anne style.

STYLE: Hepplewhite
AGE: 1785–1810
**Primary woods most frequently used:
mahogany with contrasting inlays of lighter
woods; walnut, cherry, and maple among many
rural cabinetmakers**

The straight, geometric lines of the Chippendale
period continue, but the motifs of the Hepplewhite
period—string and bellflower inlay, for example—

and the more delicate lines and proportions of the
furniture make Hepplewhite easily distinguishable
from Chippendale. There are also many innovations
in chair backs during the Hepplewhite period, and
new furniture forms—tambour desks and
sideboards—evolved during this time.

STYLE: Sheraton
AGE: 1785–1815
Primary woods most frequently used: mahogany, walnut, cherry, and maple, and other woods often used for painted furniture

Sheraton furniture is often combined with Hepplewhite and, together, called American Federal. However, there are some major distinctions between the two styles. While Hepplewhite legs are almost always square and tapering, Sheraton legs are generally round and may be reeded or plain. The preferred ornamentation during the Hepplewhite

period was inlay, but carving is the most frequently found decoration used to enhance Sheraton furniture. Note the carved legs and chair backs here.

For more detailed information on the major styles of American-made furniture of the eighteenth century, see the Bibliography.

BEGIN BY STUDYING THE RIGHT STUFF

Books are only one part of learning about antiques. They are fine reference points, but nothing takes the place of hands-on investigation of the object itself. To go a step further, the tip we cited in chapter 1 that was given by the U.S. Treasury agent—to study the original, the real—is the best advice we can give you. Once you are familiar with the "right stuff," when you see the fakes, frauds, altered and reproduction pieces you'll also see red flags.

TOO MANY STYLES

The twentieth-century secretary bookcase illustrated here combines the basic Chippendale style of a pitched pediment with glazed doors in the Hepplewhite manner above a base with ornamental split spindles and graduated ball feet of the type used during the Empire period (1830–1850).

Now, how does the experienced antiquer analyze this piece? First, when viewing the piece he identifies the three different styles and their dates: Chippendale (1755–1790), Hepplewhite (1785–1810), and Empire (1830–1850). He then reasons that the piece cannot be any earlier than the dates of the most recent, or latest, style. Since the latest style seen on the piece is 1830 to 1850 the piece could not possibly be any earlier than that.

But, he further reasons, why would someone creating a piece in the Empire period want to take component parts from two earlier styles? He wouldn't. He would want the piece to be in the newest fashion, or totally Empire. On the other hand, furniture designers who were creating new designs in the 1920s and 1930s delighted in combining any number of elements from various furniture styles to create a "new look" that was, at the same time, "traditional." That, in reality, is the origin of the secretary. It was mass-manufactured by the Rockford Standard Furniture Company of Rockford, Illinois, in the late 1920s.

So your first lesson should be to study the books

The combination of Chippendale, Hepplewhite, and Empire styles immediately identifies this secretary bookcase as a twentieth-century reproduction.

on American period furniture (read the text and look at the illustrations) recommended in the Bibliography and take every opportunity to see period pieces in museums, restorations, shops, and auctions. Then when you are face to face with a piece composed of too many styles you'll know you're seeing the "wrong" piece because you've never seen a "right" one like it.

Here's another example and explanation of a piece made up of too many styles.

Some nineteenth- and twentieth-century chair designers who were copying earlier styles must have thought, the more styles the better! When the designer of the Duncan Phyfe line at the Rockford Standard Furniture Company came up with this particular chair in the 1920s he brought together elements from four different styles. The crest rail combines Sheraton turnings along the top with a pint-size Hepplewhite interpretation of a broken pediment at the center. The back splat is a fanciful idea of a Queen Anne vase motif back, pierced in the Chippendale fashion, and the legs are turned in Sheraton style. There is no way the student of eighteenth-century American furniture could ever give this chair a second glance as an eighteenth-century chair. Yet, day in and day out, someone in our appraisal group is shown a similarly styled chair that the owner believes dates from the eighteenth century.

PIECES MADE IN THE STYLE—BUT NOT UNTIL LATER

Suites or suits of furniture as we know them today rarely existed in eighteenth-century America. True, Chippendale dining room tables were used with Chippendale dining room chairs, in the same room with a Chippendale side table and Chippendale chest. All pieces were in Chippendale designs, but in eighteenth-century America pieces were bought or commissioned one or two at a time, often from different cabinetmakers or workshops, often in different years, in different locations, and, especially in the more rural areas, even of different woods. The concept of totally matching furniture groups began with mass-manufactured pieces in the 1840s and 1850s.

By the turn of the century furniture was made to accommodate new popular forms with earlier styles. For example, sideboards were designed originally in the Hepplewhite era, beginning around 1790. If you look in any of the books on style recommended in the Bibliography you will not see a single sideboard in Queen Anne or Chippendale design before 1890. But the three illustrations on page 34 are interpretations of eighteenth-century-style sideboards. All three date from the twentieth century and were mass-manufactured in America. But these are typical of pieces sometimes thought in the 1990s to be much older than they are.

The first is a "Queen Anne–style sideboard" made by the Grand Rapids Furniture Company in 1916. Second is a 1922 Hayden reproduction more in keeping with Queen Anne features, but still, of course, a twentieth-century designer's concept. And last is a "sideboard of the Chippendale school" made in 1932 by Baker Furniture Company.

To alert you to these later forms made in earlier styles, here is a checklist of many pieces made at the turn of the century often wrongly attributed to the eighteenth century.

• Sideboards—first made around 1790—never in the Queen Anne or Chippendale periods.

*Three fanciful sideboards
made in the twentieth century.*

This idealized room scene from Modern American Period Furniture *was labeled "Chippendale style." Yet not one piece of furniture is true to the Chippendale style, nor would a true period Chippendale dining room have been furnished* en suite. *But in the 1920s and 1930s, suites of matching pieces were the rage.*

- Dressing tables with attached mirror—though these first appeared around 1800, they were never made in the Queen Anne or Chippendale periods.
- Coffee or cocktail tables—low tables begin appearing in the 1920s, which means *any* low coffee or cocktail table in Queen Anne, Chippendale, Hepplewhite, or Sheraton styling is of modern vintage.
- Case pieces with large, single-pane glass doors—especially those having a Queen Anne– or Chippendale-style base.
- Extremely small ladies' writing desks—especially those on Queen Anne bases—are almost always modern adaptations.
- Queen Anne armchairs (and settees, sofas, wooden-backed day beds)—these were made in the period, it is just that they are so rare they seldom appear in the marketplace, and if you do find a "right" American eighteenth-century armchair, look immediately at the price tag—but more about that later.
- Music cabinets on stands in the Queen Anne style—music stands became popular in the third quarter of the nineteenth century, not in the first half of the eighteenth.
- Small end tables—tables under twenty-eight inches high were introduced in the twentieth century, just before coffee tables, to suit the lower arms of twentieth-century sofas.

A good rule of thumb is to be cautious of any diminutive piece that is particularly well suited to contemporary purposes as these are more likely to

Beware of small secretaries and writing desks, dressing tables with attached mirrors, any coffee table labeled "antique," and of upholstered Queen Anne–style chairs.

Hints and tips on how to uncover evidence of this form of fakery are given in the following chapters and particularly in the individual case studies in Part Two.

SIZE AND PROPORTION

If you've ever read the captions under the photographs of items sold at estate auctions reported in *Maine Antiques Digest* (and if you're serious about American eighteenth-century furniture this should be required reading), you've seen such comments as "the size was right," or "all the proportions were right." These phrases are usually followed by a large sale price and a comment about the good buy the purchaser got.

be either adaptations of eighteenth- and nineteenth-century styles or made-up pieces.

And while speaking of made-up pieces—those pseudoantiques ingenious cabinetmakers have created by combining old parts (leaves from a table that is otherwise warped, spokes from a broken spinning wheel, the backboards from pieces where the fronts were smoke or fire damaged are just a few of an endless list of possibilities) and old wood (floorboards, shelving and other architectural remnants from buildings and houses) with new materials—here is a short list of the forms so often made up during the first part of the twentieth century and sold as period pieces.

huntboards
all hanging shelves and plate racks
lowboys and highboys
chest on frames
spice cabinets

In 1925, the Pierce-Arrow seen through the window in the background of their ad in House & Garden *cost $7,000. The little chairside table is as new and fashionable as the car. It would have cost no more than $12.50 or $15.00. Though in colonial style, small, low side tables are definitely twentieth-century designs rather than antique pieces.*

Or if you've ever listened in on the telephone conversation of an expert dealer getting the details he needs to decide whether it's worth a trip to look at an American piece being offered for sale, you've probably heard something like this:

"A chest of drawers? How wide is it? Oh? That's a little wide. Sounds like the L and U type [that's shorthand for large and ungainly] to me. How about measuring it again? . . . And by the way, make sure you measure the chest top, not just across the drawers."

Why the concern with proportion and dimensions? Because proportion, dimensions, and size are often immediate indications about both the rightness of a true American period antique and its salability. And at other times, even if a piece is right, size can affect value, as you'll see in the second example given below.

You'll find references to the importance of correct proportions in many books on American antiques, but in the step-by-step analysis following this general introductory section, you will find guidelines of actual dimensions to assist you in determining whether a piece is of the period, has alterations, or is from a later date.

But for now, as you stand back and look at the particular object you're considering, remember the following examples.

EXAMPLE 1—THE WRONG SIZE

Often when copying eighteenth-century pieces, nineteenth- and twentieth-century makers adapted the proportions of the earlier pieces to modern housing and life-styles. This concept has already been touched on under style, but a quick comparison between a period, eighteenth-century Chippendale secretary bookcase and a later reproduction shows how the proportions in some of the later reproductions differed.

A general rule of thumb is that most American eighteenth-century Chippendale secretaries are between ninety-two and ninety-eight inches tall. But many turn-of-the-century reproduction Chippen-

Some upholstered reproduction pieces can be doubly confus-ing because true period fabric was used on new frames. This new settee frame, advertised by W. & J. Sloane in 1916 as one piece in their collection of "Furniture Covered with Old Nee-dlework," was upholstered in early-eighteenth-century tapes-try.

dale secretaries measure from seventy-eight to eighty-eight inches tall, or a full ten inches shorter than those made a hundred years earlier. Why? When the middle class could afford a mass-manufactured secretary bookcase, once only found in wealthy homes, furniture designers made the necessary changes. Smaller middle-class homes made it necessary to scale down the size of the original designs to fit lower ceilings and smaller rooms.

Take a moment to glance at the illustration of this 1920s secretary bookcase (right). You probably would immediately identify it as an "adaptive" re-production, but read the description anyway. "Height, 70 inches." See how the accumulation of information can quickly make you into a more as-tute antiquer!

Once your eye is trained in the correct propor-tions of true period pieces you will also quickly recognize when specific parts of a piece are in the wrong proportion to the total piece. Most eighteenth-century pieces are ample when com-pared to their later interpretations, especially Queen Anne and Chippendale.

EXAMPLE 2—HOW SIZE AFFECTS VALUE

Even when a piece is right—right age and right size—its dimensions can affect its value and its eventual investment potential.

Who doesn't want an eighteenth-century American chest of drawers? Right now you want the chest to fit the space in your living room between two windows, but later you might want to move the chest into the foyer. And ultimately, when you can afford it, you want to get a fine antique chest for your guest bedroom. You might just get a chest now to use in the living room but plan to move that chest to your guest bedroom later and upscale the piece for your living room. Quickly you grab the tape measure and begin taking notes. You might be able to use a chest forty inches wide, but thirty-five or thirty-six inches would be much better. Once you begin shopping you find you're not alone in wanting the smaller chest. In fact, you quickly find

Gumwood was one of the exotic veneers frequently used in the early part of the twentieth century.

that the price difference between the thirty-five-inch-wide eighteenth-century New England Hepplewhite cherry chest and its forty-inch-wide counterpart is $2,000 or more! Of course the ultimate decision of which of the two you buy is a matter between you and your pocketbook, but knowing that size can affect value may help you in making your choice.

A good rule of thumb is that you can expect to pay $1,000 more for every inch *under* thirty-nine inches wide for a good, standard period chest of drawers and $2,000 more for every inch *under* thirty-six inches wide.

MATERIALS

Fine furniture always has been made out of the best quality woods available to the furniture maker. During the eighteenth and early nineteenth centuries the cabinetmakers were partly, but not wholly, dependent upon the native woods for their materials. Chapter 9 deals specifically with woods, and there you will learn much about choices of woods. Another quick reference is the inclusion of the primary woods most frequently used during each of the periods cited earlier in the section on style in this chapter (see pages 25–31).

The important point for you to learn here is what materials you *will not* find in true eighteenth- and early-nineteenth-century American period furniture that were frequently used in twentieth-century reproductions. During the late 1910s and 1920s "exotic" woods, especially elaborately grained burl (or burr) veneers, were highly touted by furniture makers. Some truly were richly figured and expensive woods, but others were porous, low-quality woods and were used on poor- to mediocre-grade lines.

Two points to remember are (1) the tools necessary to produce sheets of veneer large enough to cover sizable case pieces were not readily available in the eighteenth century and (2) even during the Hepplewhite period, when inlay was so fashionable, veneer was used in combination with solid boards (sides, tops, and so forth) rather than veneering of entire pieces.

Craftsmen used solid boards for highboys, lowboys, chest on chests, chairs, tables, virtually all the forms we cover in this book. A rule of thumb if you're offered a veneered piece, or one of exotic wood, would be to check not just these pages, but such important references as *Fine Points of American Furniture* (see Bibliography) and auction catalogs from Sotheby's and Christie's to see if other pieces of the same period, style, and form shown are ever veneered or are of solid woods.

COLOR

Chapter 10 deals with patina. No other single aspect has more bearing on distinguishing a period antique from a later piece, or antique that has been altered in some manner, than does patina. Even if a piece is genuinely of the period, but has had all its patina, that rich accumulation time creates, removed by refinishing and sanding, its ultimate beauty and value, as well as its "pedigree," have been affected. So if, when you first spy a piece, it looks "new" on the outside—no matter its age, no matter how untouched it is on the interior—if you're after a true American period find, this piece will not satisfy you.

AND DON'T FORGET THE PRICE TAG!

Don't get us wrong. There are "steals" to be had every day. Even as we were writing this chapter, we heard of one of the finest, purest, untouched huntboards—yes, huntboards are in our list of most frequently made-up pieces—that sold for $300 when its true value exceeds $3,000. The point is that the seller did not know what he had. Such situations as that put you, the expert, in the driver's seat.

Conversely, when you are in an antiques shop or stall, beware the dealer who gives you the sales pitch, "All I would have to do to double [or triple or quadruple or whatever] my money on this piece would be to send it to auction. A piece just like it sold last week for . . ." (Name your figure, but it is

A picture really can be worth a thousand words. This illustration by Howard Chandler Christy for Mrs. Humphrey Ward's popular 1902 novel Lady Rose's Daughter *tells us much. The "grandparents'" furniture is in the height of the turn-of-the-century fashion. Though in Jacobean (or colonial, as it was referred to then) style, the suite is fresh out of the furniture-store showroom. How do we know? See the mirror over the sideboard? For starters, Colonial families had neither sideboards nor long rectangular mirrors in the late seventeenth and early eighteenth centuries. The moral? Grandparents and even great-grandparents bought new furniture, too. Don't be fooled into thinking an item is truly a period piece just because it belonged to an ancestor. Scrutinize the pieces, and remember,* objects do not lie!

usually several thousand dollars more than the price he is asking for his item.) In such situations, simply ask yourself, If the piece is so valuable, why would he (or she) sell it for so little? For example, last summer I stopped into an antiques shop and was drawn to an Empire sofa roped off so no one could sit on it. Why, I wondered, would anyone be so protective of that old reproduction, which had been newly (and badly) refinished? When I saw the price tag of $5,000, I could no longer contain my curiosity. "Tell me about this sofa," I requested. The owner immediately complied not just by answering but by pulling out books showing pictures of Empire sofas, clippings from magazines featuring Empire sofas in state houses and governors' mansions, and even pages from New York auction houses of truly fine Empire sofas. None bore the slightest re-

semblance in age or quality to the $5,000 one in the shop. Then came the usual pitch: "All I'd have to do to get fifteen thousand for this sofa is to send it to New York." Of course if he had sent the sofa to New York the shipping expense would have exceeded the $200 he might have gotten on a good day at an auction *if* any auction house would have accepted the sofa for sale, and then the auction house commission would have been another $40 or so. Ironically, fine Empire sofas of the type he *thought* he had usually sell in the $10,000 to $15,000 range. The moral is simple. First, learn how to correctly *identify* American period pieces. Then follow the marketplace. Learn how much American period pieces are selling for and you will not be taken in by reproductions or altered pieces and you'll also be able to walk away with the steals.

5

Most Fakery Is Only Skin Deep: An Introduction to Period Joinery

hough the outside of any piece of furniture is important, especially the patina, to fully appreciate and authenticate American furniture it is essential to understand and analyze the details of construction. And the collector who understands construction will be far more astute and keen than the person who can only identify periods and designs. We routinely find dealers, decorators, and collectors who can wax eloquent about every style and motif but who haven't the vaguest idea about tools, woods, or construction.

Interior construction details reveal far more than do the exterior appearances, especially on those pieces that are old, faithful, measured copies of period pieces. Most fakery is only skin deep simply because the expense of creating the proper period construction details is prohibitive. Fakers depend on a prospective buyer's being mesmerized by the exterior and looking no further.

One reason antiques have survived through the centuries is the strength and durability of their construction techniques. By learning to identify proper construction, the student of American antiques can avoid purchasing a fake or reproduction.

The next few pages are filled with technical details that few readers will find breezy reading. You may need to reread this material numerous times if this is your first exposure to the inside story of furniture construction. We further suggest that you

not only read these pages but that you reread them while you are involved in a hands-on examination of various furniture forms. Remember, you may select either a reproduction or a period piece for your firsthand inspection as we guide you through what you can expect to find in either instance.

JOINT CONSTRUCTION

In order to build strength and durability into a piece of furniture, interlocking joints must be employed anywhere wood meets at right angles or edge to edge. Through the ages cabinetmakers devised several methods to achieve this end. During the eighteenth century, although their methods were time-consuming and often complicated, the result was most effective.

Later, when the industrial revolution of the early nineteenth century made machines available to cabinetmakers, craftsmen found it time-efficient to replace the handcrafted joints with machine-made joints. Fortunately for the student of antiques, these readily identifiable changes make it simple to place pieces within specific time frames. By learning to distinguish pre–industrial revolution techniques from later methods you will be able to date antiques much more accurately than if you rely on style alone.

RIGHT-ANGLE JOINT CONSTRUCTION

By the mid-nineteenth century the cabinetmaker's major concern of strength and durability became secondary to time-efficient labor methods. Thus handmade joints were soon replaced by machine-cut dowels and dovetails. The accompanying box provides a quick reference of both early handcrafted and later machine-produced methods used to make right-angle joints.

In this table the rectangular tenon slips into the mortise joint and is then securely pegged through the holes.

RIGHT-ANGLE JOINTS ON PERIOD FURNITURE

mortise and tenon
handmade dovetail
shiplapped or rabbeted and pinned joint

RIGHT-ANGLE JOINTS ON MACHINE-MADE FURNITURE

machine-made dovetail
rabbeted and pinned joint

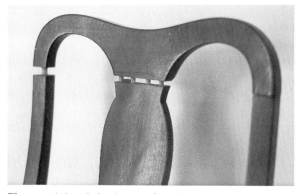

The round dowels jutting out from the crest rail are slipped into the holes of the stile and back.

Mortise and tenon. Probably the oldest wood joint known to man, the mortise and tenon joint has been found on furniture excavated from ancient Egyptian tombs and was in continual use until it was replaced by the dowel joint during the mid-to-late nineteenth century. The mortise and tenon joint should be encountered in antique furniture anyplace wood is joined at a right angle to the grain of the wood—for example, where table leg meets skirt, or where crest rail meets the upright stile. In most cases this joint is locked with a through peg. On occasion, when completely piercing the abutting member, the exposed end of the tenon will be wedged or keyed. In the finer urban pieces the mortise and tenon joint is tightly fitted and frequently is not pegged, wedged, or keyed.

Dovetail. Although the dovetail joint was also employed by the Egyptians as early as the tenth century B.C., it did not come into common use in America until about 1690 or 1700.

In antique furniture, anywhere two flat pieces of wood meet at a right angle, with matching grains end to end, the dovetail joint is most likely to be encountered. Look for dovetails where sides meet top and bottom in case construction and where sides meet front and back in drawer construction.

Unlike the mortise and tenon joint, which was most often pegged, keyed, or wedged, the dovetail joint is usually a self-locking joint where triangular tongues cut in one board are mated to triangular cuts in the opposing board. Further, the dovetail joint is probably the most visible sign of early construction. In addition to drawer interiors and the sides of chests, visible dovetails are also encountered in blanket chests and foot construction. When a dovetail is visible from one side only, it is referred to as a half-blind dovetail. Such a dovetail is fre-

Two examples of through tenon joints. The first shows a wedged tenon joint usually encountered on benches. The second shows a keyed-through tenon joint.

Dovetails are used to join flat pieces of wood end to end at right angles, as in this drawer construction.

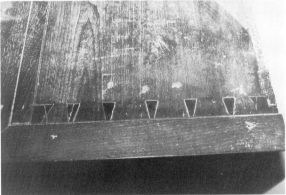

Dovetails are often readily visible in case construction. Top is a half-blind dovetail construction along the top edge of a slant-top desk. Above shows dovetail construction evident on the upper case of a desk and bookcase.

A half-blind dovetail used in case construction.

This foot construction demonstrates another use of the ship-lapped joint.

quently encountered in foot construction and finer case construction.

A little-known fact is that joints that appear to be merely mitered are actually fully blind dovetails with a mitered outer edge. The blind mitered dovetail can be found in ogee bracket feet and in the finest case construction, as in knife boxes and tea caddies. (This has been an overlooked point, as few people have seen the inside of an ogee foot.)

Shiplapped or rabbeted and pinned joint, butt joint, and plain mitered joint. In contrast to sophisticated city pieces, in many country-made antique pieces the dovetail joint is replaced by a shiplapped or rabbeted and pinned joint. Look for

This illustration shows how the simple butt joint is used to join two right-angle boards on a drawer.

A shiplapped joint may be found in the place of dovetails on some country pieces and on seventeenth- and very early eighteenth-century pieces made before dovetails came into common use.

This shows the common mitered joint used on both the lid and case of a bottle case.

this construction where you would expect to find dovetails used, in case and drawer construction and, most frequently, in foot construction.

While the simple butt joint is often found on homemade rural pieces, the common mitered joint is found on both fine and country pieces. Both are still in use today.

Machine-made dovetails. By the time the machine era was widespread, handmade dovetail joints were replaced by the machine-generated dovetail joints, of which several varieties are illustrated here.

As you will notice, the machine dovetail joint is often similar in appearance to a handmade dovetail joint. But as with all machine products, this joint is perfectly uniform; the handmade dovetail, on the other hand, will have slight but measurable variations. If you are uncertain whether you are looking at a machine dovetail or a well-executed, precise, handmade dovetail, take the time to measure the tongues. There will always be some variation if the dovetail is hand cut, perhaps just a difference of a thirty-second of an inch. Machine-cut dovetails follow a gig and will not vary.

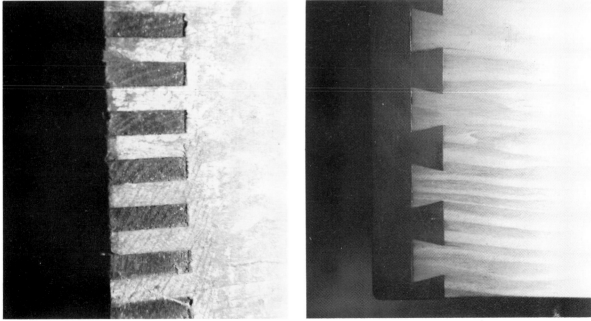

These three illustrations as well as the one at the top of page 48 represent varieties of machine-cut dovetailing.

EDGE-TO-EDGE JOINT CONSTRUCTION

Other types of joints are necessary to secure wood pieces together where they meet edge to edge. These joints occur at such places as tabletops, case sides, slant-top writing surfaces, and blanket chest lids where two pieces of wood are jointed to form a wider piece.

EDGE-TO-EDGE JOINTS ON PERIOD FURNITURE

mortise and loose tenon
butterfly bridge
tongue and groove
spline
rabbet-lapped joint
breadboard cleat
batten, nailed, or inset
sliding dado joint

EDGE-TO-EDGE JOINT ON MACHINE-MADE FURNITURE

dowel joint
tongue and groove

Mortise and loose tenon, butterfly bridge, tongue and groove, spline, rabbet lapped. Cabinetmakers employ a variety of methods when joining wood edge to edge with the grain. In antique furniture we invariably encounter either a butt joint with mortise and loose tenon, dowels, a butterfly bridge, the tongue and groove, spline, or rabbet-lapped joints. These joints are employed in table leaves, chest tops, case sides, or anywhere two pieces of wood meet edge to edge with the grain.

A blanket-chest top with butt joint secured by a mortise and loose tenon joint.

This tabletop with butt joint is secured by a butterfly bridge visible from the underside of the table. Photo courtesy of the Museum of Early Southern Decorative Arts

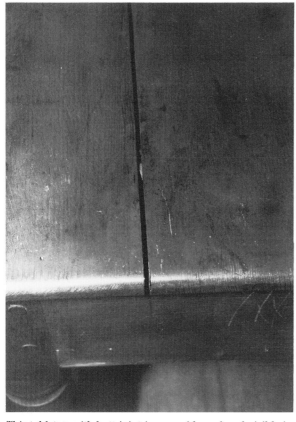

This tabletop with butt joint is secured by a dowel visible in the crack between the two boards.

Here the tongue-and-groove joint is visible from the end of a tabletop.

A double groove with spline joint visible from the end of a tabletop.

A shiplapped joint visible from the end of a tabletop.

Dowels. With the advent of machine-oriented cabinetmaking, most of these joints were superseded by the dowel butt joint identical to the earlier dowel butt joint (see page 44). But the tongue and groove and rabbet-lap joints are still in common use today.

Breadboard cleat. A breadboard cleat is frequently used to secure edge-to-edge joints—for example, the ends in blanket chest lids and tabletops. Breadboard cleats can either run the entire width of the board or be mitered on the ends. This mitered breadboard cleat is frequently encountered in fall-front desk lids and tabletops.

A breadboard cleat running the entire length of a fall-front desk lid.

Battens, nailed on or inset. Battens serve the same purpose as breadboard cleats and are either nailed on or inset in long dovetailed dado cuts placed some distance in from the ends of the top. Nailed-on battens are frequently found on country-made blanket chest lids and cupboard doors. The inset dovetail batten is usually found on more sophisticated pieces such as underneath table leaves to retard warpage or to secure chest lids and table-tops. Because the breadboard cleat and the dovetailed dado batten run perpendicular to the grain, they serve a dual purpose of joining the wood and impeding warpage.

A nailed-on batten visible on the inside of a blanket-chest lid.

A mitered breadboard cleat on an early tabletop.

A mitered-in batten visible from the front edge of a tabletop.

Sliding dado joint. When wood is joined together at right angles, as is the case with shelves, drawer dividers, or door and panel construction, a sliding dado joint is required to allow for shrinkage. These dado joints can either be cut with straight sides or tapered on one or both sides. When tapered they are referred to as dovetail dados or half-dovetail dados. Such joints are visible from the ends. When they stop some distance from the ends they are referred to as blind dados.

Though sliding dados are still used today, the dovetail and half-dovetail dado are rarely encountered in machine-manufactured furniture.

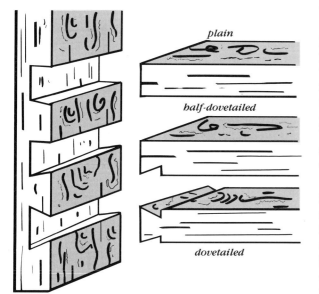

plain

half-dovetailed

dovetailed

half-blind dado

Many beginning collectors question the usefulness of this technical information about joints, especially as it is often impossible to disassemble furniture, joint by joint, to determine its age. We repeat our earlier statement that although the joinery methods of eighteenth-century craftsmen were time-consuming and often complicated, the result was most effective. In contrast, many machine-made joints loosen and slip and sometimes are readily visible to the careful examiner. Being able to identify the method of joinery on a piece may help you immediately dismiss it as a later reproduction or a piece that has undergone substantial repair or alteration, no matter how "old" it appears on the outside.

If you are really serious about purchasing a major piece but have doubts that it truly is a period piece, it is possible to have joints X-rayed. A few years ago, when a museum was offered an often faked form, we were suspicious enough, or cautious enough, to advise the museum to X-ray the joints where the stretchers and legs were united. The X ray clearly showed that the stretchers were correctly mortised into the legs, and the museum was pleased with its new, authentic acquisition.

This caution was the only reasonable route after the infamous fake Brewster chair incident, which occurred several years earlier. The positive identification of the chair as a fake hinged on X rays that revealed the sharp screw tip made by modern drill bits inside the chair members. Obviously, you don't want to waste your time or money X-raying a $225 late Sheraton side chair, but it may be worth it if you've come to an impasse on a $15,000 Queen Anne side chair.

6

TOOLS AND THEIR MARKS

Before the industrial revolution, furniture making was a laborious process completely dependent on hand-operated tools and simple hand- or foot-powered machinery. We in the twentieth century have a hard time conceiving of such painstaking procedures, but we owe the craftsmen who executed them a debt of gratitude. For like the detective who investigates the scene of the crime, obtaining hard evidence from such seemingly minor traces as footprints and fingerprints, the student of American antiques can determine the approximate age and authenticity of furniture through the "fingerprints" left by the cabinetmaker—that is, the marks made by the tools used in the construction of the piece of furniture.

SAW MARKS

The production of a single board required numerous exhausting processes before it could be incorporated into a piece of furniture. After a tree suited for an eighteenth-century carpenter's particular need was selected, it was felled by ax or crude crosscut saw. It was then cut to manageable length for removal from the forest by means of oxen or other animal labor. The tree log was then sawed into rough planks by two men working a pit-saw operation—one man above, one man below.

When a sufficient water supply was available the water-powered sash saw replaced the pit saw, reducing considerably the hand labor required for lumber production. But the procedure was still time-consuming.

A breakthrough came with the invention of the circular saw in the early nineteenth century. Tabitha Babbitt, a Shaker sister of the Harvard Shaker Community, produced the prototype of the circular saw in 1810, although it took another ten or fifteen years before it was used extensively. And not until the era from 1830 to 1840 was it in common use. It should be noted, however, that for some rural shops human labor was more readily available and cheaper than the new machine. To further conserve human labor and time a lumber operation, when powered by the newly invented steam engine, could be set up anywhere, revolutionizing the production of lumber.

Each of these saws—the hand pit saw, the water-powered sash saw, and the circular saw—left its own distinctive mark, or fingerprint, helping us to date antique furniture. The hand-operated pit saw left rough, straight marks running at varying angles; the water-powered sash saw left similar straight marks running parallel to each other. But the circular saw left unmistakable curved marks.

To find these telltale prints, look in secondary positions—drawer bottoms, runners, backs, and interiors of cases. Most cabinetmakers, past and present, try to remove all traces of saw marks by planing. But even the cabinetmaker who sets out to

The distinctly different marks made by (top) the hand pit saw, (middle) the water-powered sash saw, and (above) the circular saw are clearly visible on unfinished flat surfaces.

deceive can become lazy when working on surfaces not readily seen on first investigation. The keen observer will look in these places first.

In dating furniture by saw marks, keep these two facts in mind. First, the water-powered sash saw remained in use throughout the nineteenth century, primarily in rural areas. This means that some rural pieces may appear earlier than they actually are. The technical term used by curators and connoisseurs for the rural piece made in the later nineteenth century but in an earlier eighteenth-century style and with earlier tools is *retardetaire*. Second, the benchmark used by most experts for the appearance of circular-saw marks on urban pieces is 1830.

But most important of all, the ability to identify these different saw marks is essential to the identification of period furniture. The presence of circular-saw marks will easily unmask the fake, reproduction, or repaired antique.

PLANE MARKS

Once the log was sawed into rough planks, it had to be jack-planed smooth and the edge joints planed as well. Hand planing leaves distinctive long, shallow, slightly concave marks that most frequently run with the grain but occasionally run across the grain as well. Like saw marks, plane marks are most evident on secondary or interior positions such as drawer bottoms, backboards, and underneath tops. But even when the eyes can't perceive a hand-planed mark the hand will feel the slight ripples of planing, which can be likened to the wavy surface you feel when you run the fingers of one hand over the fingers and palm of the other hand.

Urban cabinetmakers removed plane marks from exterior surfaces with a finely sharpened straight-edge finishing plane that left an almost indiscernible mark. However, country-made pieces will frequently have visible hand-planing marks on the exterior.

Although all forms of hand planes (jack planes and finish planes) are still used by cabinetmakers today, the machine planer was introduced by the

Right: Machine planing creates shallow parallel ripples that always run against the grain.

Hand planing creates rippled, wavy marks that are discernible by feel even when located in hard-to-see positions. But if they are visible, hand-planed marks can be found running either with (most often) or against (less frequently) the wood grain.

mid-nineteenth century. Like the circular saw, the planing machine virtually eliminated the laborious hand jack-plane operation in board production. The machine plane leaves a very distinctive, yet often faint mark, quite different from the uneven, ripply marks left by hand planing. The machine plane has long blades attached to a belt-driven axle. The board cut by this machine will have a series of shallow, straight, parallel, slightly scooped marks running perpendicular to the grain.

DRILL BITS

Just as the industrial revolution changed the procedures for sawing and planing wood, it also radically changed and improved the process of tool making.

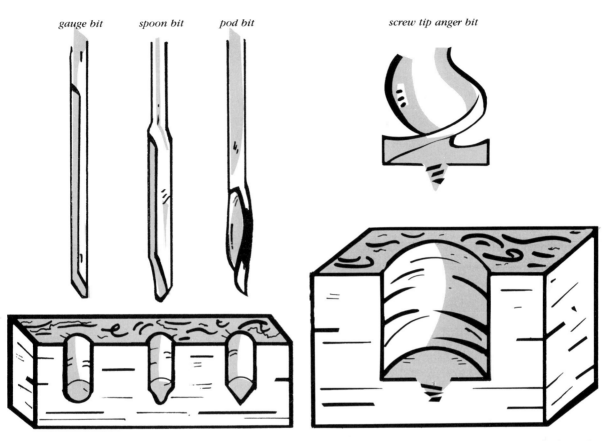

gauge bit   *spoon bit*   *pod bit*

screw tip anger bit

When X-rayed, the bottom of a hole made by a pod, spoon, or gouge bit will show up as a rounded end with no screw-tip center-point hole evident.

When a center point is evident at the bottom of a hole, the expert has evidence that a nineteenth- or twentieth-century screw-tipped auger bit made the hole.

The hand tool that changed most drastically was the simple brace, or drill bit. From biblical times on, cabinetmakers used either pod, spoon, or gouge bits. All have one thing in common. The bottom of the drilled hole is concave with little or no center-point hole evident. The new spiral screw-tip auger bit, invented by Phineas Cook of England in 1772, was a vast improvement over these old brace bits, but it cut like a pod bit, leaving a concave bottom to the hole. Apparently this invention was before its time and rarely if ever put into use.

But by the first decade of the nineteenth century, the flat-bottomed, chisel-bladed, screw-tipped auger bit was introduced and quickly accepted. (The

inventor of this bit is debated, but its first patent was placed by a man named Hoxie in 1804.) This improved bit leaves a flat-bottomed hole with a screw-tip center point that has been the conclusive mark in uncovering fakes and frauds.

The internal nature of the bottom of drilled holes makes it difficult if not impossible for the student of antique furniture to see them without an X ray. But as we noted, the famous fake Brewster chair was unmasked by X-raying its joints, which revealed flat-bottom screw-tip auger-bit marks. The presence of a concave hole with no center point evident convinced us that a piece was right for another museum.

Hand-held coping saw marks evident on the inside edge of a bracket foot.

SCROLL-FRET COPING SAW AND HAND-CHISEL MARKS

Another hand tool displaced by the industrial revolution is the scroll-fret coping saw used for sawing scalloped or scroll designs. These hand-held saws leave straight marks that usually run at various and changing angles to each other.

Flat hand-chisel marks are evident on the glue block of this foot.

The mechanized treadle-operated scroll saw of the early nineteenth century and the later mechanized band saw create similar marks, but there are distinctions. These machines leave absolutely even saw marks perpendicular to the grain. Another way to distinguish the hand-sawed scalloped edge is to look for hand-chisel marks. These scalloped edges were frequently finished or touched up by hand chisels, both flat and gouged. Hand-chisel marks are easily recognized by their unevenness. Look on the convex section of scrolled bracket feet and on the glue blocks used to reinforce bracket feet to find *flat* hand-chisel marks.

Gouged chisel marks are most frequently found on the inside of drawers where brass hardware nuts have been countersunk, under table frames where screws are inset to attach tabletops, and on the concave sections of scrollwork such as bracket feet.

Of course, both flat and gouged chisel marks are readily evident in such decorative details as carved finials and relief carving.

MOLDING PLANES

During the eighteenth century moldings were always cut by hand-operated molding planes that left no telltale marks other than the molding design itself. In contrast, the rotary-driven shaper or router that replaced the hand-operated molding plane in the first half of the nineteenth century leaves the same sort of mark as the planing machine—a slightly concave series of parallel lines perpendicular to the length of the molding. Since hand-cut moldings are cut running with the grain, sometimes the plane picks out small slivers, leaving imperfections in the molding. Cabinetmakers usually eliminated these imperfections, which are generally found only on country pieces.

Students of antiques should be keenly aware of all of these tool marks, as well as proper patination and period nails and various types of hardware. These seemingly minor details ultimately reveal the authenticity of antiques.

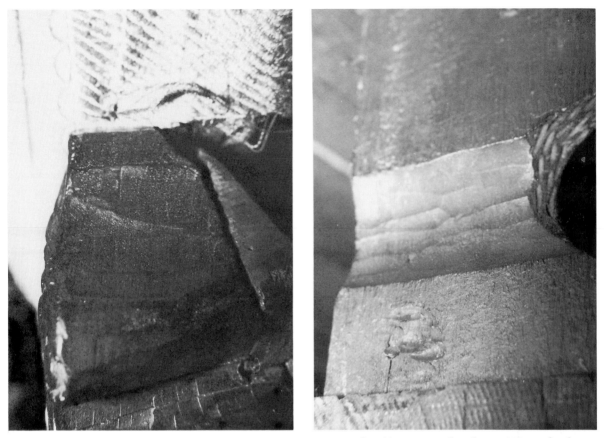

Handmade, gouged chisel marks are often found around hardware and on feet. Always remember, these two areas—hardware and feet—are essential places to scrutinize for possible replacements and should never be overlooked.

The clever faker will mask, hide, or in other ways obscure as many of these details as he can, so being able to discern just *one* detail may save you from making a costly mistake. Once we were examining a walnut huntboard that looked good in all these details except that on the back of one leg the faker had left the faint marks of a circular saw. He had gone to great lengths to fool the public by using period drawers from an old Empire sideboard and hand planing every stick of wood. But he got lazy on the back of one leg and that single slipup unmasked the deception. On closer inspection we noticed that the maker had carefully painted over fresh saw marks to the interior joints with a concoction of greenish brown paint referred to in the trade as "dirt paint." Next, close scrutiny showed the wear to the drawer bottoms did not quite match the wear to the drawer runners. The difference between the value of the correct walnut huntboard and that of the faked walnut huntboard was easily tenfold.

7

INTERNAL HARDWARE AND FASTENERS

One of the most reliable analytical tools available to students of antiques is the ability to recognize period hardware—fasteners, nails, screws, pegs, and so forth. Just as the quality and types of tools available to the cabinetmaker changed during the industrial revolution, so furniture hardware underwent evolutionary changes as newer and more efficient machines to produce it were invented.

NAILS

Handwrought nails were made by local blacksmiths or specialist nailers from the Bronze Age until the nail-cutting machine was invented sometime in the mid-1790s. The handwrought nails used in eighteenth-century American furniture were basically of two types: rosehead nails with flattened heads and finishing nails with narrow elongated heads. Two styles of ends or points exist on these handwrought nails: the pointed clenchable tip and the flattened chisel-bit tip.

Nails changed substantially in the first half of the 1790s, when the first nail-cutting machine in America produced nail blanks—that is, cut nails without heads. These blanks were then headed by the blacksmith or nailer just as wrought nails had been. These nails are identifiable by their cut shank with blunt end, which, in cross section, appears slightly angled on two sides (rhomboidal).

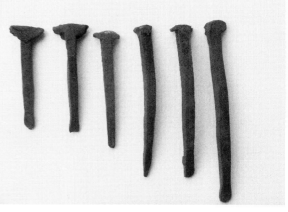

Three handwrought rosehead nails. Note the hammer-beaten shanks and irregular heads.

Several varieties of handwrought finishing nails—T headed and half-T headed.

Improvements in the nail-cutting machine quickly evolved, and by about 1798 half-T fully cut finishing nails and sprig nails were introduced. By 1805 the nail-cutting machine was capable of creating a headed nail, which could be transformed into a finishing nail simply by flattening one side of the nail head to form a T-head nail. As seen in the illustrations, these early cut nails tend to have a swell toward the top of the nail when viewed from the side. By 1820 the slight swell tends to be less evident and by the mid-nineteenth century is almost nonexistent. Of course, handwrought nails did not suddenly disappear when square-cut nails appeared.

The accompanying box can be used as a general guideline for identifying and dating nails.

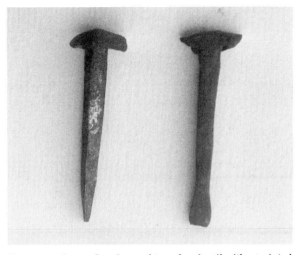

For comparison: a handwrought rosehead nail with a pointed clenchable tip and a handwrought T (or finishing) nail with a flattened chisel-bit tip.

- **Handwrought nails were used until around 1810.**
- **Square-cut nails were used from 1800 until about 1890.**
- **Wire nails with round shanks became common in 1890 and are used today.**

You may wish to extract loose nails from furniture to examine the head, shank, and point. But a better technique is to examine the wood around the nail. If the wood is evenly patinated and shows no sign of having been disturbed, you can conclude that the original nail is in place. Removal of a nail, even a loose one, disturbs the wood.

Another way to investigate for later nails is to look carefully for evidence of more than one set of nail holes, especially on backboards, which have often been reinforced. If you find square- or rectangular-shaped holes along with more recent round nail holes it becomes clear that the back has either been resecured or that an old piece of wood has been used in making up an "antique." If this is your suspicion, use the appropriate case study in your investigation of the entire piece.

Cut nails truly transformed the furniture industry. Not only were they inexpensive and plentiful, but carpenters and cabinetmakers found that these new, smooth, uniformly shaped nails meant less wood splintering, a problem caused by rough, ir-

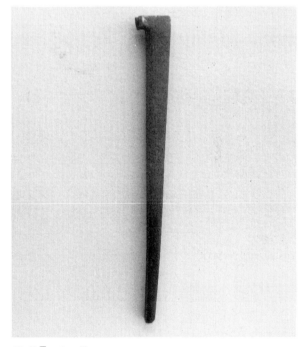

Half-T cut nail.

regular wrought nails. The one drawback to cut nails was that, at first, they were brittle, so wrought nails will still be found on pieces made in the mid-nineteenth century where a clinched nail was needed—primarily on hinges and doors made by

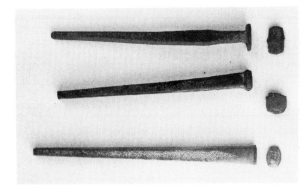

The top nail is an early-nineteenth-century cut nail with swelled shank. The middle nail is a mid-nineteenth-century nail with straight tapering sides. The lower nail is a modern cut nail. Note the smaller heads of those nails presently made.

carpenters more often than by cabinetmakers. But by and large, after 1810, machine-cut nails were used in virtually all furniture making.

Cut nails remained in use in America until about 1890, when the modern round-shanked machine-made crest wire nail was introduced from Europe. By the end of the nineteenth century the wire nail had driven the cut nail out of use for the most part. However, cut nails have remained available for specialty purposes and can still be bought at your local hardware store. But as the illustration shows, not only are modern cut nails usually of highly tempered steel, they are rather different from earlier nineteenth-century cut nails. Their sides taper uni-

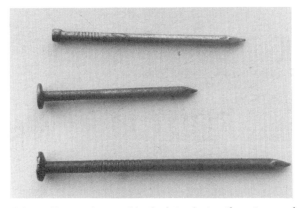

Wire nails were invented in the late nineteenth century and are still used today. Headless finishing nail (top); headed sinkers (bottom).

formly to a blunt point and the heads are rather small with less overlap when compared to the earlier cut nail. And one final comment on cut nails. In the late nineteenth century, a cast nail resembling a cut nail was introduced. Still available to a limited extent, this nail has a square head with a very distinctive round, domed top.

Cast domed-top nail.

NAIL USE

As important as knowing the different types of nails is knowing *where* eighteenth-century cabinetmakers used them. Many a fake or altered piece has been discovered when nails or nail holes were found in the wrong places.

In eighteenth-century pieces rosehead nails are primarily found in secondary positions—used to attach backboard and drawer bottoms. They are occasionally found in exterior positions in case construction of rural or country pieces.

Finishing nails, either T, half-T, or headless, are primarily used in exterior positions to attach moldings and in fine case construction. Sprig and small finishing nails are often found in fine case pieces in secondary positions, such as the small drawers of desk interiors.

Once introduced, between 1790 and 1800, cut nails were adapted to the same sorts of usage as wrought nails. You will find square-headed cut nails where rosehead nails would have been and cut finishing nails in exterior and finely fitted interior positions.

The wire nails of the later nineteenth and twentieth centuries occur in only two forms—headless

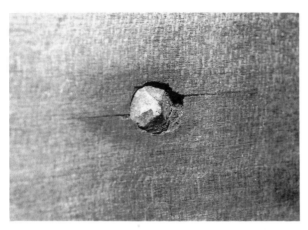

A rosehead nail in position, its head showing on a backboard.

This T-head nail is being used as a fastener to attach the tabletop to its base.

This cut nail is being used to secure a drawer bottom.

round finishing nails and round-headed common nails. Round-headed common nails, though rarely used, can be found in secondary positions, and headless finishing nails are found in all exterior positions and most interior positions.

We cannot emphasize enough how important analysis of the nails used in antique furniture is to the serious collector. So here is a hypothetical case to show how this knowledge can help you date, authenticate, and detect repairs and restorations in an "antique."

You have found a fine, eighteenth-century walnut chest of drawers that at first seems immaculate, if slightly overrefinished. On close inspection you find the backboard and drawer bottoms are attached with wrought rosehead nails, as they should be. But the bracket feet are fastened with square-headed cut nails. The fine, applied molded edge of the top at first seems to have no nails, but on closer inspection small, round, putty-filled nail holes are noted.

Conclusions:

• The basic carcass of the chest is from the eighteenth century.

• The feet have been replaced sometime in the nineteenth century.

• The molding was added as an enhancement in the twentieth century, using wire finishing nails.

• The twentieth-century enhancer refinished the chest, obscuring the differences in color and patina in these three different parts and giving the chest a uniform appearance.

• Most important, the presence of these two later additions to the eighteenth-century body decreases its value drastically, perhaps as much as 70 percent or more, and the piece is now a decorative rather than a period antique.

SCREWS

Screws, fasteners commonly found in twentieth-century furniture, are rather infrequently encountered in antique furniture, and then usually in high-stress areas, where tabletops are attached and to secure much-used hardware.

Because spiral screws have more gripping power than nails, they can better withstand the strain that comes from constant use and wood shrinkage. For this reason, wood screws were sometimes used to attach tabletops, which are apt to be affected by shrinkage. On tabletops, wood screws were used underneath the frame so fasteners are not visible from the top. This is why it is important to examine all antiques from beneath, where the true evidence of age and construction are found.

As you probably know, hardware—in particular, hinges—is fastened with screws. By being able to identify and date screws used to attach hardware you can distinguish cleverly replaced hardware from true period hardware. Many a made-up piece has slipped by dealers and collectors who saw old hardware but didn't examine the screws used to attach it.

Once you know how many tedious steps went into producing just one screw, it is easy to understand why they were used only when necessary in the eighteenth century. The blacksmith first made the round blank. Next he headed the screw, much as a wrought nail was headed. The blank was then threaded by hand with a file and finally the top was slotted with a file or saw.

Eighteenth-century screws are identified by the handwrought shanks, hand-filed threads, blunt tip,

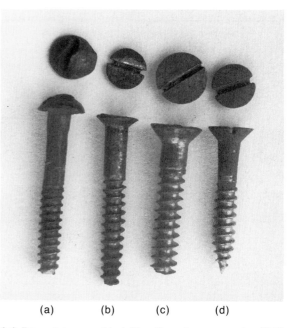

(a)   (b)   (c)   (d)

(a) Dome-top wrought eighteenth-century screw, pre-1800. (b) Flat-headed, early-nineteenth-century screw, 1800–1815. (c) Flat-top, machine-threaded screw, post-1815. (d) Modern screw with point tip.

and frequently off-center slots on either domed or flat-top screws.

About 1800 this slow hand production was expedited when the hand-cranked screw-thread spindle was introduced, a device similar to those found in tap and die sets today. The screw head, however, was still hand wrought. Thus, though the threads on screws used between 1800 and about 1815 will appear quite uniform, their handwrought heads will be immediately identifiable.

The first screw-making machine, introduced sometime around 1815, revolutionized screw production. These early nineteenth-century screws have a smooth, machined shank, even threads, and blunt tip. But the slots were still hand cut and are frequently off center.

The modern screw machine, patented in 1846 by T. J. Sloan, produces the same basic screws we use today. Modern screws have an even machined surface, pointed tip, and well-centered slots. With this invention, screws became quite inexpensive and began to show up in places they would not have

Here is a screw visible from the underside of a table set in a gouge-chiseled niche. Screws used to attach tabletops should never be visible from the top, except in some obviously rural pieces.

been used in the eighteenth and early nineteenth centuries—backboards and drawer bottoms. As a rule of thumb, remember that screws should appear only where tabletops are attached and on hardware. When found in other places ask yourself, "Are the screws added as a strengthening device or are they an indication that the piece dates after the mid-nineteenth century?"

PEGS

The wooden peg, or trunel (tree nail, as it was frequently referred to in earlier times), was probably the earliest form of fastener, predating biblical times. In eighteenth-century construction, pegs are

A fascia board with exposed peg on a Moravian kas.

These pegs secure unseen mortise and tenon joints that hold the drawer frame to the table stile. Notice the slightly elliptical shape of the raised pegs.

most commonly encountered as fasteners for right-angle mortise and tenon joints on rural-made pieces. Pegs were seldom used to secure mortise and tenon joints on finely made urban period pieces, where cabinetmakers produced better-crafted, tighter-fitting joints. Remember also that once inexpensive mass-produced screws and dowel joints became available in the mid-nineteenth century, few cabinetmakers, except those in truly rural areas or those producing homemade furniture, would have continued to make and use wooden pegs.

But there are exceptions to that rule of thumb. For example, pieces of Germanic influence—in particular, Pennsylvania and Piedmont Southern furniture—frequently exhibit pegged case construction. On these pieces pegs were used to fasten backboards and drawer bottoms as well as to attach fascia boards in cupboard and chest construction.

In rural-made furniture pegs will also be encountered where table and chest tops are attached to the bases. Here pegs will be readily visible from the top surface.

The collector can usually trust the presence of pegged construction as a sign of genuine age when all other evidence is correct. The major exception is

Pegs used to attach a chest of drawers' top in place, unlike screws, will be visible from the top.

those handcrafted reproductions of the early twentieth century frequently pegged in imitation of the earlier work. But most of the pieces will exhibit circular-saw marks, the wrong kind of nails or screws, or some other evidence of their true origin. But when examining wooden pegs remember that, viewed from the top, most eighteenth- and nineteenth-century pegs are not truly round. To make a tight fit, cabinetmakers would use a slightly square peg in a round hole. As a result, the finished peg, when flush with the surface around it, will

This slightly raised and elliptical peg is correct and evidence of the age of this cupboard.

appear slightly elliptical or squarish. Furthermore, on pieces that have not been refinished, pegs tend to work themselves out of the hole by as much as one-sixteenth to one-quarter of an inch, due to shrinkage. Invariably, twentieth-century handmade reproductions will use round pegs cut from dowel rods that do not exhibit any irregularity. Because their "fit" is right, these pegs will generally remain flush with the surface of the piece.

Knowing this, should you encounter peg construction where the pegs are absolutely round, there is no shrinkage, and the peg heads are absolutely flush with the surface—be leery.

GLUE BLOCKS

If you remove a drawer from an eighteenth-century chest, turn a case piece upside down, or lift a slip seat from a chair frame, you may find simple wooden blocks, called glue blocks. Because these blocks were usually cut from plentiful native woods, being able to identify original, undisturbed glue blocks can help establish whether a piece is American or English, from New England or the South (see chapter 9, page 81).

As used by eighteenth- and early-nineteenth-century cabinetmakers, glue blocks had two primary functions: to reinforce areas of great stress and to secure right-angle joints.

Because they provided extra strength and reinforcement, glue blocks were especially important in high-stress areas of furniture such as seat frames and foot construction. They are encountered on virtually all bracket-footed pieces and were essential in chair-frame construction.

When used to secure right angles on tables and chests, glue blocks are found beneath the tops, where they were utilized to secure the top to the piece. Glue blocks serve this same purpose on drawers and are often found on the underside of drawer bottoms. Glue blocks were frequently used by cabinetmakers of the eighteenth and early nineteenth centuries to secure the right-angle joints in case and drawer construction, particularly on fine, urban pieces. Here they serve the dual purpose of

Glue blocks used in chair seat-frame construction.

Glue blocks used to reinforce the right-angle joints of a straight bracket foot.

Glue blocks used in the inside of a table frame to help secure the right-angle skirt joints.

functional construction while reinforcing drawer-bottom joints.

Because glue blocks were often weight-bearing parts and frequently had to be replaced over the years, it is important, for two reasons, to determine whether they are original to any given piece. First, if the glue blocks are original and *undisturbed,* you can be sure that the part or joint to which they are attached is also original to the piece; for example, if the top to a chest is secured by glue blocks, in order to remove that top for repair or replacement the glue blocks must also be removed. Second, glue blocks are often used by fakers to hide new parts. Some fakers will use old, patinated glue blocks from other pieces to give a fake that "old" appearance. Knowing these two facts, you realize you must be able to recognize when a glue block is original to a piece.

Hide glue, the type used in the eighteenth century, hardens over time and crystallizes, and the adhesion between the glue block and the part to which it is secured can be lost. When this happens the glue block is often permanently lost or replaced. In either instance the shape of the original glue block will leave a ghost image of lighter colored, unoxidized wood. This image *must* be present on both parts where the glue block was originally in place. If the image is present on one side of a chair frame and not on the other, you have proof that the side without the image has been replaced. The presence of undisturbed, original glue blocks indicates a piece has not been abused over the years.

On the other hand, if you suspect old glue blocks have been replaced after a new part was added, or have been used to conceal the signs of new construction, such as saw marks or screws, you should know that glue blocks tend to take on the same patination or color as associated secondary woods. The collector should always be suspicious when encountering obviously new glue blocks or glue blocks that have been stained or painted over, or that appear unusually large or are present in an unlikely place. However, new glue blocks that have been added in the place of old, lost glue blocks are not considered a serious restoration.

Knowledge of glue blocks can add up to dollars

Glue blocks used to help secure a drawer bottom.

The glue block has been lost on this bracket foot. Notice the ghost stain left by the lost block. Compare this with the middle illustration on page 65, where the blocking is intact.

saved. Once we saw a rather fine New England cherry dishtop tea table. At first glance the table seemed fine. The underside patina was right. But the two-board top glued in the middle and secured with a rather large oblong block looked suspicious. This seemed an unusual placement for a glue block, so we cautiously recommended that the block be X-rayed. When the X ray came back it clearly showed that the block's purpose was to cover a table hinge scar. The conclusion was that the top now on the base had originally been the top of a drop-leaf table that had been reshaped and re-carved to become a dishtop. Taking the time to think through the unusual placement of the excep-

tionally large glue block and follow up the suspicions with the help of modern technology revealed a made-up piece. Had the table been correct, its value would have been in the $30,000 range. With its new top, its value was reduced to $2,000.

A final word of warning. Fakers will often use glue blocks to hide the inside joints and edges of replaced bracket feet. This frequently occurs when the new, dressier feet will turn a simple $1,500 chest into a more desirable, high-style $6,000 chest. These blocks will often be stained to blend in with neighboring patinated secondary wood or even be slapped over with dirt paint.

8

EXTERNAL OR DECORATIVE HARDWARE

*D*uring the eighteenth century, furniture hardware evolved technically and stylistically; thus, knowing and recognizing the "right" decorative hardware can help in authenticating and dating furniture.

Because furniture hardware can be easily removed, many eighteenth-century pieces will have later nineteenth- or even twentieth-century hardware that was put on when the original hardware wore out or went out of fashion. But the presence of eighteenth-century hardware on a piece does not guarantee that the piece itself is as old as the hardware. Sometimes early hardware is put on a nineteenth-century piece or twentieth-century made-up piece when the intention is to pass off the piece as being older than it really is.

One of the first questions we hear beginning collectors ask antiques dealers is "Are the brasses original?" To the experienced collector, the absence of original brasses does not devalue a fine piece. But when the original eighteenth-century hardware remains on a piece, its value is almost always substantially higher than the value of a comparable piece that has replacement hardware.

For these two reasons—authenticity and value—the serious collector will learn how to determine whether the hardware is original to the piece or is a later replacement. In most cases, this is a fairly simple procedure.

BRASS DRAWER PULLS

Drawer pulls are usually fastened to drawer fronts with screws or staples that completely penetrate the drawer front. These pulls are anchored with nuts, or, in the case of staples, are folded over and cleated in the inside surface. By simply looking at the inside surface of a drawer front you can determine if the pulls are the first set by the number of holes left by a previous hardware set or sets.

This simple test becomes difficult when the first set has been replaced by a later set using the same holes. At this point you must rely on a more technical analysis of the hardware itself and its components.

Though your first instinct may be to remove the hardware and examine it for technical differences that will establish its age, take a moment to look further at the outside of the hardware. Brass drawer pulls that have never been removed from a piece of furniture usually exhibit a continuity of color and patina. On the other hand, when brass pulls have been removed from the piece of furniture for polishing, scratches to the surface and dents to the nuts often occur. If you conclude that the original pulls are present and have never been removed, *do not* remove them now. But when scratches and dents are evident, then it is safe, even recommended, that you remove the brasses for further investigation.

The nuts fastening the brass posts in place are set into gouge-chiseled holes. These brasses have never been removed or disturbed.

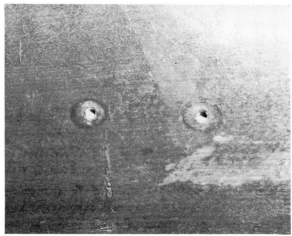

The ghost image left by a bail and rosette pull that has been removed.

A nut fastening the brass post in place, set into a gouge-chiseled hole. Note the scratches and dents to the nut indicating the brasses have been removed at some point—probably for polishing.

Once the brasses are removed you will then be able to establish whether you are looking at brass hardware that is

> original to the piece
> an early replacement
> a later replacement but using old brasses
> a contemporary reproduction

Once a pull is removed, begin your investigation by looking at the drawer front itself. Old brasses invariably leave a ghost image matching the outline of the original set. If the image differs from the shape of the brass you have removed, the present pull is a replacement. When no image is evident once the brass is removed the piece has been harshly refinished at some point and the patina and stain removed. (In chapter 10 patina will be discussed at length.) At this point, be alerted that the loss of old patina removes "fingerprints" that add up to proof of age.

Though original hardware on eighteenth-century pieces is not essential to most collectors, its presence is highly desirable, and because it can be a means for dating and authenticating a piece, here is a survey of furniture brasses as they evolved through the eighteenth century.

A GUIDE TO PERIOD HARDWARE STYLES

EARLY QUEEN ANNE HARDWARE

The earliest hardware of this period, that used on American furniture between 1710 and 1720, was actually a holdover from the William and Mary period and will be rarely encountered. This hardware is usually teardrop pulls attached by staples, often referred to as snipes. Be warned that during the last part of the nineteenth century, almost two hundred years later, teardrop pulls became fashionable once again and were used on almost every style of furniture. On true early Queen Anne hardware the staples will pierce the drawer front and be folded over and cleated in the interior. Later American teardrop pulls will be screwed on. (The English did produce fake, staple-type pulls, but our concentration here is on American furniture.)

As the Queen Anne period became established (1720–1760), the bail-pull handle with a simple shaped backplate, frequently referred to as a batwing pull, was introduced. These pulls are usually plain, but some are engraved and even pierced. During the early part of this period, 1720–1730, the snipe or staple method of attachment was still used to secure the hardware to the drawer. But toward the middle of this period the threaded post with nut was introduced. These early brasses are quickly recognizable by their crudely threaded posts, which were hand cut, and the assymetrical nuts used to secure them.

An engraved teardrop pull found on William and Mary as well as on some very early Queen Anne furniture.

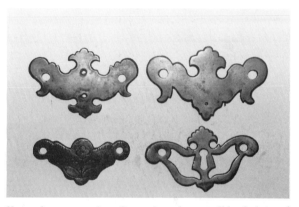

Shown here are various Queen Anne brass pull backplates of the batwing type. Note that some are solid and some have open work as well as engraving.

The staple fastener used to secure teardrop and other early Queen Anne brasses, as seen on the interior of the drawer.

Queen Anne batwing pull shown with its posts, nuts, and bail.

CHIPPENDALE

During the Chippendale period (1760–1790), bail handles generally became larger as more elaborately shaped backplates evolved. The design of the backplate is often referred to as the willow pattern and, in some cases, the backplates are elaborately pierced as well. It is important to know that engraved backplates are no longer encountered. The fastening post also became heavier and, in most cases, a little less crude in appearance during this time.

Toward the middle of the eighteenth century, the popularity of the large backplate began to fade as the new bail and rosette pull became popular. This style of hardware is frequently encountered on pieces from 1750 through the first decade of the nineteenth century, or until around 1810. It is often possible to distinguish between eighteenth- and nineteenth-century rosettes. Eighteenth-century rosettes of the 1750–1780 period are cast, whereas later eighteenth- and early-nineteenth-century rosettes are often stamped from sheet brass.

Also encountered on some high-style mid-eighteenth-century Chippendale pieces are elaborate rococo bail and rosette pulls. And then, late in the Chippendale period, around 1780, ring pulls with a single threaded post were introduced. This type of hardware is most often found on the later, transitional Chippendale pieces and on furniture made during the Hepplewhite and early Sheraton periods.

HEPPLEWHITE AND SHERATON HARDWARE

During the later eighteenth and early nineteenth centuries, brasses went through some extraordinary stylistic and technical changes. Oval and rectangular backplates, stamped from sheet brass, were introduced. And a decorative top was introduced on the previously utilitarian fastening post. Also during this period the biscuit knob, a hollow, stamped brass sheet knob and backplate with single-threaded shank, was introduced. These are

Chippendale willow-pattern brass pull backplates of both the solid and open-work varieties.

A Chippendale willow-pattern brass pull shown with its fasteners and bail.

A bail and rosette pull shown in place. Note that the tops of the posts are molded.

Both fronts and backs of rosettes used with bail pulls are illustrated here. The top row shows the backs and the bottom row the fronts. The left two rosettes are cast and the far-right rosette is a later variety stamped from sheet brass.

A rococo bail and rosette pull.

most often decorated with geometric and figural designs and remained popular into the late Empire period.

WHAT TO LOOK FOR

HAND-PRODUCED PULLS

Pulls made during the late eighteenth century, on into the nineteenth century, found on Hepplewhite and Sheraton furniture can be correctly identified by collectors once they learn what to look for.

- Posts, bails, backplates, and rosettes that were hand cast in sand will have small pits and anomalies on the surface, normal indications of the sand casting.
- Hand-threaded posts will show considerable irregularity and unevenness.

A brass-ring pull handle with attached sand-cast fastening post is on the left with its stamped sheet-brass backplate on the right.

The stamped sheet-brass biscuit knob, its backplate, and the single attached fastening post.

Several varieties of stamped sheet-brass backplates commonly encountered on Hepplewhite and Sheraton furniture.

These stamped sheet-brass biscuit knobs show the variety of designs used to decorate the knob faces.

The tops of brass-pull fastening posts. The two plain posts on the left are from the Queen Anne and Chippendale periods. The two molded top posts to the right are late-eighteenth- and early-nineteenth-century types.

Compare the left column of antique fastening posts and nuts with the right column of reproductions. Note the difference in the surface texture and threading between the two columns. From top to bottom the left column shows period Queen Anne, Chippendale, and Federal hardware.

• Fastening nuts, both those cut from cast sheet brass and those that were hand cast, will have very irregular shapes.

WARNING

Many of the fine details that help distinguish period brasses from twentieth-century brasses are evident in the best of today's handmade reproductions. However, careful examination of the posts and nuts can reveal minute differences. On twentieth-century reproductions the threading of the posts will be more regular than on period posts, and the nuts are also usually cast with greater regularity and thus will have sharper edges and smoother surfaces than earlier, hand-cast nuts.

The fastening nuts on the top row are antique, while the nuts immediately below are comparable reproduction nuts.

OTHER HARDWARE FORMS

HINGES

Wrought-iron hinges. Identifying the material and form of hinges—an essential fastener for doors, lids that open, and table leaves—can assist the collector in correctly dating and knowing the origin of furniture. A helpful rule of thumb is that during the earliest part of the eighteenth century most hinges were wrought iron. By around 1730, brass hinges replaced wrought-iron hinges in urban areas. However, wrought-iron hinges were retained in rural cabinet shops throughout the eighteenth and well into the nineteenth centuries and thus are often found on retardetaire and provincial pieces.

The most frequently encountered wrought-iron hinge forms are the snipe or staple hinge, the butterfly hinge, the H hinge, and the strap hinge.

The snipe hinge is the simplest and, dating from medieval times, the earliest form of hinge. On American furniture it is found on country pieces throughout the eighteenth century and into the early nineteenth century.

Wrought-iron butterfly hinges are usually an in-

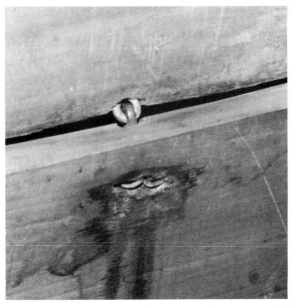

This double-staple, or snipe, hinge is in place on a period blanket chest.

dication of seventeenth- or early-eighteenth-century construction and are rarely encountered past the first quarter of the eighteenth century.

On the other hand, wrought-iron H hinges were introduced in the early eighteenth century and were used extensively on country furniture until about 1800. The wrought-iron H hinge is most frequently encountered on pine pieces and painted cupboards and chests.

This wrought-iron butterfly hinge is an outside fastener on a New York State kas.

This strong wrought-iron strap hinge was designed to take the constant use given to blanket-chest lids.

Wrought-iron hinges are most frequently used on rural pieces. Here an H hinge appears on a pine corner cupboard.

Finally, wrought-iron strap hinges, although encountered on early-eighteenth-century cupboards, are predominately a chest-lid hinge. Examples will be seen on pieces dating from the seventeenth century through the late eighteenth century. During the third quarter of the eighteenth century the strap hinge was often replaced by the cold-rolled smaller and more uniform fish-tail strap.

Brass hinges. Introduced in the early eighteenth century, brass H hinges were used on the fine furniture of the period until the end of the century, when they were replaced by brass butt hinges.

The earliest brass H hinges were frequently scal-

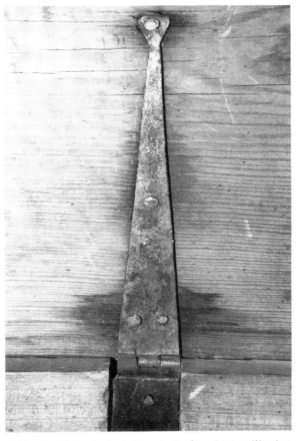

Cold-rolled fishtail strap hinges are found on utilitarian country pieces such as this blanket chest.

On this walnut corner cupboard the cast-brass H hinge is a step up from the wrought-iron hinges found on many pine pieces.

loped and fastened with a single screw on each half with a small nail at the tips. But when the plain H hinge was introduced by 1740, screws were usually used to fasten the hinge to the wood. It is relatively easy to determine when hinges have been replaced. Because hinges take a lot of abuse over the years, old hinges will show considerable wear on the spines, whereas later (replaced) hinges will show little wear.

The brass butt hinge was introduced in the mid-eighteenth century and is usually encountered on fine urban cabinets. By the late eighteenth century the cast-iron butt hinge was introduced, but it is usually found only on more rural or utilitarian furniture.

Wear is visible on the spine of this hinge. Also note the gap that has evolved with constant wear.

A cast-brass butt hinge shown front and back.

Two nineteenth-century cast-iron butt hinges. Notice the rough texture of the surface of the older one pictured at left.

A wrought-iron table hinge.

Table hinges. During the later William and Mary and early Queen Anne periods, the butterfly hinge was used to attach table leaves. But by 1730 the specially wrought-iron table hinge was developed, to be superseded by a cast-iron hinge of the same form by the late eighteenth century. The difference between these two hinges is easily detected by observing the wrought, hammer-beaten surface versus the smoother, cast-iron surface.

ADDITIONAL HARDWARE FORMS

Small specialty pulls. Small brass pulls or knobs are often found on small drawers, primarily in desk interiors or drawers on miniatures, and on the slides that support the writing surfaces or fall-front boards on desks. The earliest knobs have oval or ovoid tops and were used on furniture from approximately 1700 through the middle of the century. Introduced during this same time frame were the more common plain knob distinguished by its slightly curved crown and the plain ring pull. These were used throughout the eighteenth century and well into the nineteenth century.

Yet another type of small pull found on these interior drawers and slide supports is the shaped drop pull. Introduced early in the eighteenth century, this form was seldom used after the first decade of the nineteenth century.

Note the hand-threaded shank on this early-eighteenth-century ovoid top knob.

A late-eighteenth-century ring pull and curved crown knob.

Compare the eighteenth-century knob with the hand-threaded shank shown at the left with the reproduction knobs on the right. Note the uniform threads and pointed tip on the far right reproduction.

Both forms, knobs and drop pulls, made during the eighteenth century will have hand-threaded screw shanks, making them relatively easy to distinguish from later reproductions that have machine-threaded shanks.

Tilt-top table latches. Latches used on tilt-top tables underwent stylistic changes during the eighteenth century, and knowing the evolutionary differences can be useful in determining the age of a tilt-top candle stand or tilt-top tea table.

On more formal furniture, brass-cased tilt-top table latches appear as follows:

earliest period   1720–1740
middle period   1740–1810
later period   1785–1830

Drawer locks shown front and back.

Local blacksmiths made wrought-iron latches used by rural cabinetmakers.

Wrought-iron tilt-top table latches appear on more rural pieces and can take numerous forms as they were made by local blacksmiths whose abilities varied.

Locks. The locks used on doors, drawers, and pieces with lids remained fairly similar in outward appearance throughout the eighteenth century. But as you become more familiar with the various hardware forms, you will observe that, externally, the earliest locks are cruder and larger, while later locks are more compact and streamlined.

Until the third quarter of the eighteenth century, cabinet and drawer locks were relatively expensive. As a result, the earlier eighteenth-century cabinetmakers used locks only on some drawers. For this reason, rarely will you find locks used on *all* the

A typical fall-front desk lock shown front and back.

A cupboard door lock, front and back.

A blanket-chest lock with catch.

drawers of a chest of drawers. But by the later eighteenth century, or roughly the last quarter of the century, and early nineteenth century, locks were routinely used on all the drawers of a piece. This is why you may encounter some drawers that have the outward appearance of a locking device, but find upon opening the drawer a solid, uncut drawer interior.

Locks will vary in form according to their purpose. Among the forms you can expect to find and illustrated for you here are:

drawer locks
fall-board locks
cupboard door locks
blanket chest locks with catch
blanket chest grab locks

Through the text and illustrations of chapters 7 and 8 you now have a guide to the identification and dating of internal and external hardware. But remember our warning: Hardware, being separate from the furniture piece itself, can, has been, and will continue to be removed and used to distract the potential buyer from other, more important and telling signs of deception and age.

Ultimately, just how important is the hardware? Use as your guide not only the information in these two chapters, but also the references given in the case studies in Part Two.

Hardware is only one part of the total puzzle that comprises the hunt for the great American furniture treasure.

9

WOODS

The primary woods, those woods used by cabinetmakers for furniture exteriors, can tell us much about where the piece was made and its relative age.

You may have heard that once the primary wood is known, it is possible to determine a piece's origin. This information can be helpful, but because primary woods were routinely exported from heavily forested countries and shipped all over the world, it is the secondary wood, or that wood used in the interior (drawer bottoms and sides, backs of cupboards) that is of most importance to the student of eighteenth-century American furniture. Almost always, the eighteenth-century cabinetmaker used native woods for interior construction. For this reason, if you are interested in correctly identifying regional furniture, and most serious furniture students eventually evolve to this point, it is essential that you possess at least a casual knowledge of woods and their origins.

We will quickly add that wood identification can be both difficult and confusing. Even experts can be fooled by woods when a snap identification must be made by the naked eye—particularly when there is a great deal of money on the line. The following story illustrates why it is important to understand primary and secondary woods and how their identification can mean the difference in thousands of dollars.

We once saw a rather desirable small thirty-four-inch-wide walnut chest of drawers with a writing slide, the type often referred to as a bachelor's chest. The dealer selling the chest said it was obviously English because the secondary wood was oak. However, the dealer's asking price was $6,000—an exorbitant price for an English chest *of this sort.*

Upon examining the chest, two points disturbed us. First, the form and construction were more typically American than English, and second, the secondary woods were all lightly patinated. English furniture usually has a very dark, almost black patina that develops over the years as a result of the coal the English use for heating their homes. On truly antique and old English pieces the years of coal soot will build up a very dark, distinctive patina, especially on the backboards and the bottoms of case pieces.

Though he was taking a chance, Joe decided to buy the chest on pure instinct. Then came the hard part—the task of proving through wood analysis that the chest was, indeed, American, and worth at least four times the value of an English chest.

Oak, although not commonly used in America as a secondary wood, does occur with considerable regularity along the Eastern seaboard. Experts in the field are familiar with the heavy use of oak in shipbuilding and point out that cabinetmakers probably bought their planks from shipbuilders to use in the interior construction of furniture. In this case, microanalysis established, without question, that the oak used as the secondary wood was white oak, grown both in England and America and microscopically indistinguishable.

Further, when analyzed, the primary wood in the chest was found to be American walnut. But American walnut was actually exported to England during the eighteenth century, and thus he felt that more definitive proof had to be established.

At this point he went back to the chest, hoping to find that some woods other than oak and walnut might have been used in building the piece. In this particular chest, long, paneled dividers or dust boards were present between the drawers. It was obvious these were a soft wood in the pine family—American juniper or white cedar perhaps? But the tests concluded this wood was spruce, another wood commonly found in both American and English (as well as Canadian and European) furniture. By this time Joe was totally frustrated but still determined.

Back he went to the interior of the chest, looking for yet another specimen of wood—he hoped, American. Then he noticed that one of the dust boards had a slightly different grain pattern from the others. And when he looked carefully at the glue blocks under the top board of the chest, as well as those securing the feet, he spied a wood that appeared to be tulip poplar. So this time three samples, one from the dust board and one from two different glue blocks, were sent off to the lab for analysis. This time the tests showed that the two glue blocks were indeed American tulip poplar and that the wood used for the dust board was Atlantic white cedar. Both of these woods are positively American woods. But better yet, Atlantic white cedar only grows along the Eastern seaboard from New Jersey to North Carolina. This information, combined with detailed stylistic analysis of the construction and style, related this chest to the Williamsburg and Norfolk area of Virginia. And its value? Today, about $15,000.

Because similar situations frequently arise, if you have a particular problem with wood identification and the time to seek professional help, there are several laboratories that will microscopically analyze and identify wood samples for you. Don't just send off a sample. Write first for information and guidelines. One such laboratory is Forest Products Laboratory, 1 Gifford Pinchot Drive, Madison, Wisconsin 53705-2398.

Several fine books devoted entirely to the study of woods are available for detailed study. After studying the introductory information provided here, the beginning collector should consult the Bibliography for further reading.

THE MOST COMMON AMERICAN FURNITURE WOODS

Numerous varieties and specimens of woods were used in eighteenth-century American cabinetry. But there are twenty that you should strive to become most familiar with.

Apple, a pinkish fruitwood, frequently figured with wide bands or streaks of darker coloration, is hard and dense-grained and has no visible pores. Used as both a primary and secondary wood throughout the Eastern seaboard, apple is frequently hard to distinguish from cherry and other fruitwoods. This confusion is compounded by the distinctive rays on quarter-sawed pieces that are identical to the naked eye to those rays also found on cherry and maple.

Apple

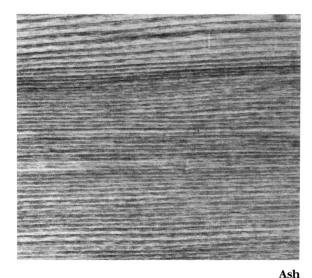

Ash

Beech

Ash varies in color from gray to white and is usually identifiable by its coarse, straight graining with clearly visible open pores. Ash was most often used in turnings, such as chair and table legs and stretchers, but it was occasionally used as a secondary wood in larger case pieces, particularly in the urban New England and mid-Atlantic regions.

Beech is light tan when freshly cut, but can age to a deep amber color. A hardwood, its tight grain and distinctive ray pattern make it more easily identifiable than some other light woods. Because beech was a favorite wood among English chair makers in the eighteenth century, many people associate it with England. Two points need to be made. First, because wood-boring insects are much more common in England than America, a quick rule of thumb when there is not time for further analysis or investigation is that beech pieces showing extensive bug damage are more likely to be of English than American origin. Second, though beech was infrequently used in America, it will occasionally occur in American furniture as the choice for upholstered chair frames and turnings in beds and chairs.

Birch, a light tan wood with a relatively straight close grain, was commonly used as both a primary and secondary wood throughout New England. A southern variety, the red river birch, can be found

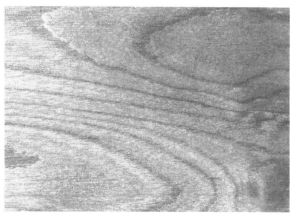

Birch

in some mid-Atlantic and Southern furniture, usually as a primary wood. Quarter-sawed birch often exhibits a fine curly figure, almost satiny in appearance, much like the figuring of curly maple.

Butternut, a pale tan color, having an open coarse grain with prominent pores, is frequently confused with light-colored walnut. In fact, it is often called white walnut. Butternut, however, is much softer than walnut and its grain is usually straighter with larger visible pores than those found in walnut. If it is possible to test a piece, butternut, being more porous, is more easily split than walnut. A quick, on-site test can be conducted with your fingernail.

Butternut

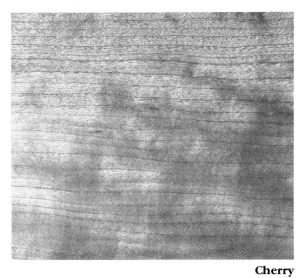

Cherry

Relatively softer butternut can be dented with your thumbnail whereas walnut usually cannot be. Another test is, if the end grain is visible, you will see a distinctive lustrous sheen. You can remember this by associating the luster or shine with butter. Only butternut and spruce give off this luster. Butternut was used as both a primary and secondary wood throughout the Appalachian range from New England into the Deep South. For this reason, most pieces with butternut will be distinctively regional pieces, in contrast to the pieces characteristic of the urban centers along the Eastern region of the same states.

Cherry, which can range from light to medium red in color, is a moderately hard wood and rather close, straight grained with almost invisible pores. Though it was used as a primary wood in New England, it was also used throughout the country in the eighteenth century. In fact, it was considered a choice wood by eighteenth-century cabinetmakers. When quarter sawed, cherry will exhibit a distinctive ray pattern and occasionally large, curly figuring, not unlike maple.

Chestnut is white to light tan and is distinguished by its coarse, open grain with prominant pores and its complete absence of rays. Chestnut appears most frequently as a secondary wood in eighteenth-

Chestnut

century pieces from Rhode Island and New England, but also occasionally in pieces made in the Piedmont region, ranging from Pennsylvania to South Carolina.

Gum, a pale yellow wood with a fine closed grain, is relatively soft. Though used as a primary wood in New York and the mid-Atlantic region, and occasionally for Southern furniture, gum was a cheap wood used for rural, painted pieces and architectual elements. For this reason, sweet gum is seldom encountered as a "finished" wood, but when quarter sawed, gum exhibits a distinctive stippled figure. It is important to know that gum takes finishes exceptionally well. According to Walter Keller, a wood specialist, pieces made of gum can have a mahogany or walnut finish and be undetectable except to the expert. Fakers have known this for years.

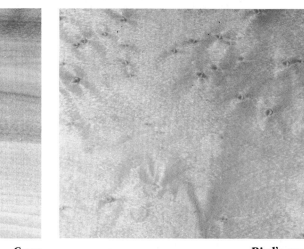

Gum   **Bird's-eye maple**

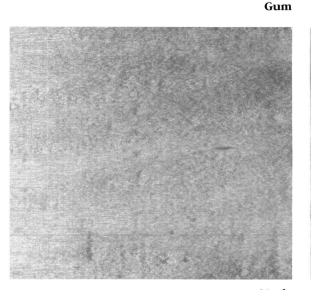

Maple   **Curly maple**

Maple can range from pale tan to light amber and is a very hard wood with a faint grain and few visible pores. Exotic figuring is evident on selected quarter-sawed maple boards. Furniture of either curly maple or bird's-eye maple is favored by many collectors. Furthermore, maple can have a distinctive ray pattern similar to the ray patterns of cherry and apple. Maple was a choice primary wood among eighteenth- and early-nineteenth-century New England cabinetmakers. But it was common through the mid-Atlantic region and to a lesser degree was used in the South as well.

Oak varies from white to tan in color and is distinguished by its coarse, open grain, which exhibits prominent pores. Quarter-sawed oak, so easily recognizable because of its predominant use in the late nineteenth and early twentieth centuries, has clearly visible rays that run throughout. Oak was rarely used as a primary wood in American furniture after the first decade of the eighteenth century, but it is occasionally encountered as a secondary wood in structural case construction in urban areas along the Eastern seaboard. To confuse matters, oak was the preferred secondary wood of urban English

Oak

White pine

cabinetmakers and was also a popular primary wood among English rural cabinetmakers. However, do not automatically dismiss a piece as English just because you identify the secondary wood as oak. Look further for other secondary woods such as white pine, Atlantic white cedar, or tulip poplar, often used as a secondary wood in combination with oak, that may identify the piece as American.

White pine, a white to light-tan softwood, has a pronounced veined pattern that accents its straight grain. When white pine ages it develops dark rays parallel to the grain, a feature that helps distinguish it from the multitude of American and European softwoods of similar appearance. White pine is the most frequently encountered secondary wood in eighteenth- and early-nineteenth-century New England furniture. And it was also used as the primary wood on rural furniture that was to be painted. White pine was extensively exported from New England and as a result occasionally occurs in mid-Atlantic and urban Eastern seaboard pieces.

Yellow pine ranges from light tan to amber and its much stronger dark veining reveals a distinctive straight grain more pronounced than that of white pine. Harder than white pine, yellow pine is relatively straight grained and often quite resinous. Yellow pine is the secondary wood most commonly

Yellow pine

encountered on pieces made south of southern Pennsylvania and New Jersey, although small amounts of yellow pine are found in Connecticut furniture of the early eighteenth century.

Cypress, tan to dark amber in color, is a relatively soft wood having dark veining with a very tight, straight grain. Cypress splits easily and, like yellow pine, is often quite resinous. With oxidation, cypress changes to a gray-black color on exposed areas such as backboards and bottoms. Cypress is frequently encountered as a secondary wood on pieces from the coastal Deep South and does not appear on furniture made elsewhere.

Cypress

Atlantic white cedar, or **juniper,** varies from light to medium tan. Its light veining reveals a barely discernible, relatively straight grain. Easily split, this wood is commonly confused with Scotch pine. During the eighteenth century Atlantic white cedar was used almost exclusively as a secondary wood along the Atlantic coast from New Jersey to southern North Carolina.

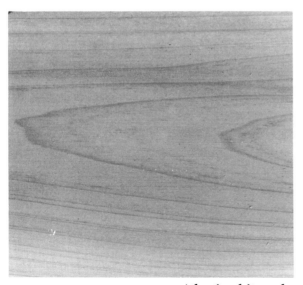

Atlantic white cedar

Scotch pine does not occur in American furniture, but because it looks so much like Atlantic white pine, many English pieces with this secondary wood are mistakenly thought to be American. For this reason it is important for you to have some knowledge of Scotch pine. Its color ranges from white to light tan with medium veining that shows up its straight grain. One way it sometimes can be distinguished from Atlantic white cedar or juniper is through the presence of small, round knots having a distinctive black bark ring. When these are present, Scotch pine can be differentiated from other pines, spruces, and junipers.

Scotch pine

Spruce, a very soft white to light-tan wood, has light veining with an indiscernible grain. Frequently numerous small, round knots surrounded by light, brown-black rings—yes, that's right—similar to those found in Scotch pine, will occur. Because spruce was used as a secondary wood all over England and Europe, as well as in Canada and along the Appalachian mountains in America, when you encounter a piece that could have spruce *or* Scotch pine as its secondary wood, you may wish to proceed cautiously if you are interested in purchasing only American furniture. Again, spruce and butternut are the only two woods that emit a lustrous sheen across the end grain.

Spruce

Mahogany ranges from light tan to the darkest amber in color and can also vary from a soft, easily pierced wood to an extremely hard, dense wood. The grain of mahogany is easily visible on the better grades and will vary from straight lines to finely figured, almost satiny swirls. The best-quality mahogany can be identified by its hard, dense surface and its richly figured grain, which is often accented by color variations ranging from light to dark within the same piece of wood. This fine mahogany, so valued by eighteenth-century cabinetmakers, was imported from the West Indies and can be further distinguished by the presence of small white flecks in the grain when it is freshly cut by a knife. Of course, this on-site procedure must be exercised with great caution and always with the permission of the dealer or owner of the piece. Sometimes mahogany can be difficult to distinguish from walnut. However, the presence of small, closely grouped or dense pores can help differentiate mahogany from richly figured walnut.

Tulip poplar can range from a light tan to a dark brown color, but a distinctive greenish cast is frequently present. A relatively grainless wood, without any visible pores, tulip poplar is sufficiently soft that it can easily be dented by your fingernail. Tulip poplar was second only to white pine for use as a secondary wood among eighteenth-century American cabinetmakers. And it was also used extensively in architectural and rural cabinetry that was to be painted. This spongy, grainless wood actually holds paint better than any other softwood. Because tulip poplar is found from southern New England into the Deep South, and is unlike any of the European poplar trees, its presence is considered to be an almost infallible sign of American-made furniture.

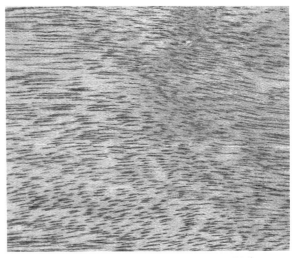

Mahogany

As you may already know, there are many varieties of mahogany, and it grows in locations throughout the world. In the eighteenth century, just as today, mahogany was exported from the tropical forests of Africa, Latin America, and Asia to England, Europe, Canada, and America. And then, as today, mahogany was the most common primary

Tulip poplar

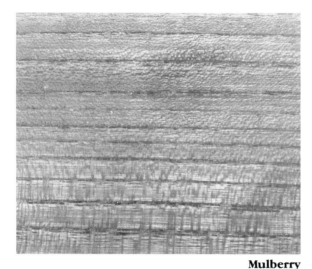

Mulberry

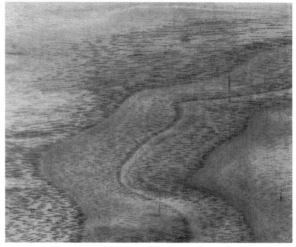

American walnut

wood used by urban furniture makers. Besides its rich figuring and color, mahogany is preferred for its resistance to insect damage, and when properly seasoned, it rarely warps and shows very little shrinkage.

Mulberry can begin life varying from light tan to a dark, reddish-brown color, but over time it patinates to a very deep, almost burgundy reddish brown. A hardwood, almost impervious to bug damage, mulberry has a coarse, straight grain speckled with visible open pores. When a board of mulberry is cut across, these pores appear as broad rays. Many people are familiar with mulberry trees as the home for silkworms, which live on the leaves and spin their valuable cocoon on its limbs. Because of their value in the textile world, mulberry trees were exported from the Far East in the eighteenth century to America. When mulberry occurs as a primary wood in American period antiques it is almost always in chairs and tables. Mulberry was often used for country slat-back chairs and occasionally for table-leg turnings. It will show up as a secondary wood, but rather infrequently.

American walnut is found in a variety of shades of brown from light tan to very dark chocolate. The grain varies as well, ranging from rows of straight grains to rich, figured designs, and the open pores are immediately visible. A hardwood, walnut is not easily dented, one of the reasons it was a favorite primary wood for both urban and rural cabinetmakers in the eighteenth century. In the Southern colonies, particularly North Carolina and Virginia, walnut was often used as a secondary wood. Be warned, however! American walnut was so plentiful throughout the eastern section of the United States, ranging from southern New England through Pennsylvania, down into the Deep South, that it was exported to England and Europe during the early to mid-eighteenth century. For this reason, the presence of American walnut does not assure that a piece is necessarily of American origin. Further, the English and Europeans have their own varieties of walnut, which can create further confusion. The visual differentiation of American walnut from other walnut can be difficult. However, a rule of thumb is that American walnut is far less susceptible to insect damage, thus the signs of extensive boring or other insect infestation usually precludes an English or European origin. When there is sufficient time, microanalysis will easily establish the type of walnut and should be relied upon when no conclusive secondary woods are present in the piece.

10

SURFACE DETAILS: SHRINKAGE, PATINA, AND FINISH

*E*ven after wood has been treated, worked, finished, stained, and has become just one board in a large piece of furniture, it continually moves, shrinks, and expands in response to its environment. A humid environment causes wood to expand, resulting in swelling and warpage; a dry environment causes wood to shrink, resulting in cracking, splitting, and the eventual misalignment of joints. In most instances, over many years of varying environmental changes, especially in modern homes where air conditioning and heating dry out the air, wood will become dry and shrink.

SHRINKAGE

Under these conditions, wood most often shrinks naturally across the grain, rather than with the grain. The result of this shrinkage is best illustrated by measuring a round tabletop and discovering that it is now slightly elliptical. Though the circle was cut perfectly round in the eighteenth century, through time as much as three-eighths- to a three-quarter-inch difference may have occurred. Denser mahogany shrinks less than does cherry, for example, but even in mahogany, often a difference as much as one-quarter to three-eighths of an inch will be noted. Therefore, it is safe to assume that a perfectly round tabletop (candlestand, tea table, or tavern table) *cannot* date from the eighteenth century and is either

an outright fake
a reproduction
its top is a replacement

The same sort of shrinkage occurs on turned elements—chair legs, stretchers, and spindles. These, too, over the years, will shrink from being a perfectly round circle to a subtle elliptical shape. Sometimes this is evident to the naked eye. Sometimes it will be noticeable by feel if you grasp a "round" element between your thumb and first or second finger. But, of course, the surest test is the careful use of calipers—a technique discussed in all books on understanding furniture. Whatever method you use, remember to check round elements carefully as many stretchers, legs, and spindles have been replaced over the years.

Another point to know is, anytime one piece of wood is joined to another piece of wood at a right angle, such as is found on breadboard battens on desk lids or mortise and tenon framing joints, there *should* be a slight misalignment of the joint or a crack. This is another natural occurrence that comes slowly over the years.

As wood shrinks with time, flat surfaces, most obviously tops and sides, develop a slightly uneven, undulating surface. A perfectly smooth surface is an

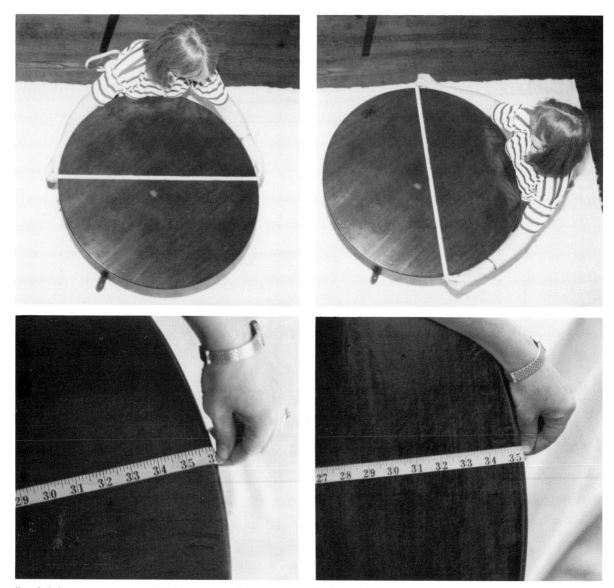

For shrinkage, measure round tabletops across the grain and with the grain. This eighteenth-century mahogany tilt-top table measures 35⅞ inches with the grain, but 35⅜ inches across the grain.

indication that the piece may have been harshly refinished or sanded.

When looking at case construction where the sides are securely joined—the most obvious example is dovetail construction—you realize that there is no room left for natural expansion and shrinkage, "breathing." The result is often a split or crack that develops on the ends or top of the surface wood where there is room for these processes to occur. If the crack is not too marring, this is generally considered a positive sign, an indication of the authenticity of a true antique, and it should not negatively affect the value of a piece.

The misaligned joint is a natural outcome of aging.

To the serious collector, a natural crack can be the telltale sign of a true antique.

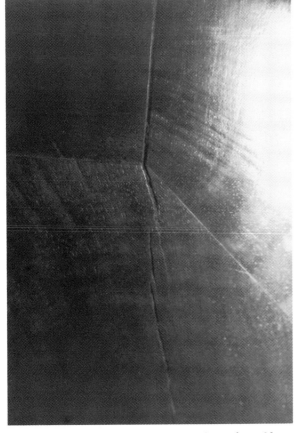

Cracks will naturally appear where two pieces of wood have been joined, as here on a tabletop. The crack comes from constant swelling and contraction as the wood reacts to its environment.

PATINA

When speaking of American period furniture, it's impossible to overstress the importance of patina. Most novices have a difficult time understanding patina and its role in the identification and authentication of furniture. Yet the "right" patina is one of the most sought after details connoisseurs search for. The buildup of dirt and grime dismissed by the beginning collector is the same mystical patina cherished as that unmistakable golden glow of beauty that can even be the experienced collector's prime reason to collect.

The sophisticated collector understands that patina is the accumulation of dirt, wax, soot, and oxidation on the finish, embellished by occasional spills and dents, that, over the years, combine to age and mellow a piece until the allusive golden aura that comes only with time emerges. Throughout the twentieth century copiers of eighteenth-century styles, from the painstaking faker to the fully mechanized manufacturers of mass-produced furniture, have strived to reproduce the natural patina that gives fine antiques the distinctive look of age. Though many have come close, none have succeeded, as *proper* patination is unfakable.

Once patina is fully understood and appreciated, it becomes the collector's best analytical tool. In fact, for some highly knowledgeable and sophisticated collectors, patina can become the most important tool for identifying and distinguishing fine American period antiques. When the eye becomes trained to recognize true, natural patina, this tool becomes infallible in determining what elements of an antique are original and what elements are later replacements or repairs. And patina can even give clues to the origin of some pieces.

Now that you understand how important patina is, let's proceed with the lesson.

In a piece of furniture, as the different wood parts (even woods of different types) age, a fine layer of patina appears over all exposed and unexposed areas. One expert dealer friend of ours, when analyzing a piece of furniture, will frequently refer to all the original patinated elements as "old friends," meaning they all share the same life span and have been in constant association. Further, patina is so thin and delicate that virtually any major or even minor repair, restoration, or enhancement will disturb it in some way.

INTERIOR PATINA

Of course, the exterior patina on an untouched piece can immediately attract a knowledgeable, experienced collector. Because chances are greater that the exterior has been refinished but the *interior* left untouched during the past two hundred years of eighteenth-century furniture life, let us begin by examining what goes on "inside" before passing judgment on the "outside."

You already understand that examining the interior or underneath of any piece of furniture is absolutely essential. Here you find new or old tool marks, fasteners, and so forth. It is also here that the patina develops ever so lightly over glue blocks, runners, and secondary woods. For example, the replacement of a top, the loss of glue blocks, or any repairs to the case become evident when different colors emerge, indicating the disturbance or absence of the otherwise perfect continuity of the in-

Perfect continuity of patina seen on the bottom of a banquet table.

terior patina. Illustrated here is the underside of a Southern banquet table exhibiting the perfect continuity of patina over its entire underside. Although the top is mahogany, the rails are poplar and yellow pine, and the legs are walnut, all four woods exhibit the same tone and color of patination. Furthermore, the screws connecting the table leaves are undisturbed, otherwise the wood would be scratched and scuffed, which would *disturb the patina.*

For comparison, also illustrated is the bottom of a New England slant-top desk that has undergone

Unscratched and undisturbed wood.

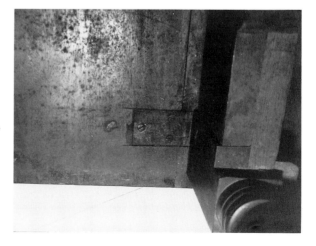

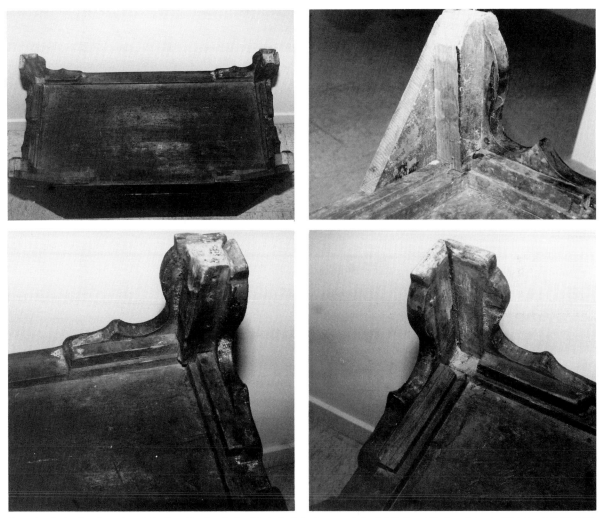

Counterclockwise from top left, New England slant-top desk bottom; original left front foot; original right front foot with replacement blocks; new, replaced right rear foot.

repairs in an attempt to blend these newer elements with the older patina. The left front foot retains its original blocking and patina. The right front foot, which is also original to the desk, but the central block has been lost, shows an abrupt change in the patina where the smaller replacement blocks have been stained in an attempt—unsuccessful, you will note—to simulate the original patina. The right rear foot has been totally replaced by using old wood that was partly colored to blend in with the patina.

Note how the stain runs down along the block and along the lower edge. The difference in color between the face and edges of the blocks and brackets is obvious. Further, twentieth-century wire finishing nails are also evident in the foot and back bracket. But even if they were not, the change in the patina should be sufficient warning to the potential purchaser.

This walk-through shows how repairs and restorations, even deceptions, can pass unnoticed without close scrutiny.

Patina can even be a measure of the caliber of the faker's art. Fakers are judged primarily by their ability to produce a believable patina that will mask new woods and modern tools, and the care they take with it is evidence of their understanding that it is the most sought after of all elements. Though true, time-built, and untouched patina cannot be duplicated, the work of the best fakers can be almost undetectable. So be forewarned that you must examine a piece inside and out, always on the lookout for a single, slight slipup. Some museum and auction-house floors have been crowded with fakes that, as yet, have not been detected.

Here are a few pointers to help alert you to some of the signs of fake finish or patina.

- *Paint and stain found in secondary positions* (drawer backs and bottoms and the backs of feet and/or glue blocks). Eighteenth-century cabinet-makers rarely painted or stained these elements. The presence of paint or stain on these elements indicates an attempt to cover over something.
- *A murky gray patination on the underside.* A common trick is to paint the entire underside of a piece with formaldehyde and then place it under heat lamps, which produces an allover gray patination. It also tends to fuzz the surface of the wood. So if you see a uniform grayish patina on the underside you can bet fakery is involved.
- *A uniform brownish patina on maple, oak, or walnut, where varying natural colors or striations should be present.* Another method is to give pieces a tannic-acid bath for the purpose of creating an allover, uniform false patina. However, tannic acid reacts differently on hard and soft woods and it tends to raise the grain in varying degrees on pine, oak, and walnut. So be leery when confronted with a piece where different woods have raised grains in differing degrees and possess an allover brownish coloration.

The best fakers will use several methods to produce a false patina. They may start with tannic acid, then smoke the piece with a bee smoker, add fake fly stains and insect holes, and finally even give the entire surface a light glue wash and powder it with fine dust, actually gluing dust onto the surface. Next obvious minor repairs will be added, such as a glue block put on without any attempt to "fake" it. This is intended to draw the unwary collector's eye to this repair—and away from the deception. Deceptive work of this sophistication is hard to detect and has fooled even the most knowledgeable curators and collectors. Unfortunately, this last statement may make some potential collectors want to "toss it all in" and seek a safer realm in which to satisfy their collecting habits. It is not our intention to scare anyone away, for there are many wonderful, even as yet undiscovered finds in American period furniture. But the *wary* collector is the *cautious* collector who will use his or her judgment to the fullest and make the wisest choices.

EXTERIOR PATINA

Just as patina is an indispensable analytical tool in studying interior or unexposed areas of an antique, it is also indispensable when analyzing exterior or exposed areas. Exterior or primary woods develop the same continuity of color. The finish, waxes, and use and wear over the years, as well as the environment surrounding a particular piece, contribute to this continuity. If a piece has been refinished at some time in its life and, in particular, sanded in the refinishing process, all traces of exterior patina will have been removed. At this point, the discussion of patina becomes moot. However, if sections of the exterior surfaces remain untouched or have been only lightly refinished—without sanding or, God forbid, dipping—then the patina remains a viable point.

Though the original elements of a piece of furniture are the same age, some parts will undergo more natural wear than others. For example, table-tops and stretchers receive more normal wear than do side rails and the legs on the same table. Taking wear into consideration, all elements of a piece should exhibit the same color, finish layers, and overall patina. In order for a faker to patch or replace an element or part on an antique he will need to match the wood grain and color, as well as the wear and finish of the layers in the surrounding areas. This is an almost impossible task. Therefore, after the required changes have been made, the faker will mask his work in one of two ways: (1) the entire piece will be totally refinished or bleached, or (2) the entire piece, or possibly just the replaced element (tabletop, stretcher, etc.), will be stained to camouflage the alterations.

The accompanying illustrated text is a mini-course in how experts use evidence, or lack of evidence, of patina in their analysis. In the first illustration note the continuity of color between the frieze and door in the upper case of this secretary bookcase. The expert then checks the lower case and carefully notes the continuity of patina between the veneered drawer fronts and solid-wood drawer blade, bead molding, and the foot. Here the expert also notes the slightly heavier buildup of the patina in the crevices and corners.

On the New England slant-top desk the patches around the lid hinge are clearly visible (see photograph at right). Note that the color and grain variation reveal more than just an obvious repair but are evidence of different patina, making the potential purchaser skeptical and anxious to look further. Observing the two right side feet (see page 96, top), the expert immediately tells from the patina that the front foot is original but the back foot is a replacement. Note the wear and buildup of the finish on the original foot and the lack of same on the rear foot, as well as a color difference. Also note the small, round filled-in holes covering the heads of twentieth-century wire finishing nails.

The photograph below shows a masterful repair of a drawer lip on a walnut blanket chest. The grain and patina are rather convincingly matched. Only a slight variation in color and grain gives this repair away. In fact, if we didn't personally know the repair existed, we would not have seen it without the aid of a high-powered magnifying glass in ideal lighting.

FINISHES

Finishes are an integral part of the patina. In essence they are the glue that holds the upper layers of patina to the surface and the lens through which the mellowed and oxidized wood is viewed. Great attention currently is being paid to "original finish" by dealers and collectors. However, determining whether the old finish on a piece is actually the original finish or merely a hundred-year-old finish, or the accumulation of as many as ten thin finishes applied to the piece over the last two hundred years, involves highly scientific skills. And even then there may be disagreement. Thus this sort of conclusion is best left to scientists and curators in museums and academic circles.

What *is* important to the collector is the *quality of the patina,* which is enhanced and preserved over the years when an old and possibly original finish still exists.

In order to detect an old or original finish the collector should first note the undulating rippling surface. Next, be aware that different finishes tend to oxidize and "age" differently. An old varnish finish often develops a network of small cracks called crazing, which resembles the spreading rays of a cracked eggshell and is sometimes seen in china. Shellac can pool or run into puddles, resulting in thinner and thicker areas of finish. Early wax and oil finishes frequently pool in the same manner. And all three types of finishes tend to accumulate in cracks and crevices. (Old shellac and wax finishes readily dissolve in alcohol, whereas varnish is more crystallized and not easily dissolved in alcohol.)

It should be obvious to the astute observer of wooden furniture that original finishes *will not be evident* on chipped areas or scratches. When such defects are present, scrutinize these areas to detect differences in color and thickness of finish. But look very closely and carefully as new finishes have often been applied directly over an old finish. If this occurred, the chipped or scratched area will have a thinner layer of finish than the surrounding unblemished areas.

Original or old finishes should never be removed. It goes without saying that the finish holds the patina. If the old finish is rough and unsightly, an experienced conservator can patch, clean, and otherwise enhance an original finish while bringing out and enhancing the best patina possible for a particular piece.

During the nineteenth century many pieces were finished over in a black ebonizing varnish that hides all beauty inherent in the wood. Such finishes, although old, frequently mask the beauty of a fine piece. Once again, the knowledgeable conservator can remove this upper finish and preserve much of the older or original finish and patina beneath.

A final word of caution. When you encounter an old accumulation of finishes, or an original finish, realize the greatest potential beauty as well as monetary value lies within this thin outer surface. Always proceed slowly and seek good, competent advice before deciding how to best preserve and restore an old finish.

11

REPAIRS AND RESTORATION, ALTERATIONS AND ENHANCEMENTS

REPAIRS AND RESTORATIONS

When talking to beginning collectors about the technical aspects of authenticating or buying antiques, the subject of repairs and restoration frequently arises. The novice's first response always seems to be, "This is just too complicated!" followed by, "Oh, well, does it really matter? After all, these things are over two hundred years old! It's understandable that they couldn't survive time's cruel hand totally unscathed."

Our response to these rationalizations is, Yes, it really *does* matter, and, yes, many items *have* survived time's cruel hand—if not totally unscathed, at least without major restoration and repairs that substantially lower their value. Specific distinctions can be made to determine when a piece has undergone too much restoration ever to be considered a wise purchase—and you will learn these points in the case studies in Part Two—but a certain amount of minor repair and restoration should be expected and is acceptable, even to the purist. In fact, sometimes minor repair and restoration are considered guidelines to true age and authenticity.

TO BUY OR NOT TO BUY

As we approached the question, "How much repair is acceptable?" or, turned around, "How much

repair is too much?" we found the answers complicated by the fact that individual taste and purpose must be factored into our technical analysis of any piece. Then, to top it all off, there is also the question, "How do repairs affect value?"

In an attempt to deal with these questions we offer some general rules of thumb, which, though not set in stone, have been seriously thought through.

The complete replacement of any major element of an antique will render it undesirable. Examples (not all are listed):

- a replaced fall board of a desk or secretary bookcase
- the replacement of one entire drawer front on any piece having *exposed* drawers (this would not be the case if a drawer front at the interior of a desk were replaced, for example)
- all four feet replaced
- the replacement of a cornice of a case piece

On the other hand, repairs or patches to any of these areas, or, say, the replacement of one foot or part of a molding, will constitute *acceptable* restoration. An exception occurs when there are *several* small or minor repairs throughout a piece, adding up to excessive restoration that, in total, becomes major. Check the case studies in Part 2 carefully and you'll soon find you're able to identify what is and what is not acceptable repair.

To get specific, let's begin by using a hypothetical piece of furniture, a nicely proportioned thirty-seven-inch-wide walnut Philadelphia chest of drawers, c. 1780, with a molded oblong top, fluted quarter columns, and ogee bracket feet to illustrate several different states or levels of repair, and then we'll conclude with our opinion.

• This hypothetical chest with its original finish and brasses and more or less undisturbed surface has a value of approximately $24,000.

• The same chest with minor restoration of replaced brasses and lightly refinished surface has a value of approximately $16,000.

• The same chest with replaced brasses, but rather harshly refinished, though otherwise original: $10,000.

• The same chest with replaced brasses, harshly refinished, having numerous small minor patches and two back feet replaced: $6,000.

• The same chest with replaced brasses, harshly refinished, with numerous small patches and all feet replaced: $3,000.

Seeing the cold, hard facts of how repairs and restorations affect a piece monetarily, you now undoubtedly agree with us that repairs do matter. And you probably also agree that determining the extent to which repairs affect value is a complicated matter, rife with disagreement and argument, centering on personal experience and individual taste.

Rarity is also a factor that affects just how much is too much. And even popular trends, usually begun by life-style magazines and coffee-table books, can affect the economics of supply and demand. When demand exceeds supply, many people will settle for more repair or alteration than they should. You see, when *everyone* wants our hypothetical Philadelphia Chippendale chest, someone will have to settle for the $3,000 version after the $6,000, $10,000, $16,000, and $24,000 chests are all gone. Knowing this, many a shrewd dealer will raise the $3,000 price tag a couple of thousand dollars and still find a buyer—but usually that buyer is a novice.

But before you accuse today's antiques dealers of promoting and selling fake, made-up pieces, deceptions—whatever you want to call them—remember that many pieces were altered fifty, seventy-five, and even one hundred years or more ago. Take the time to read the ad from Tiffany Studios that appeared on the back cover of the November 1915 *Arts and Decoration* magazine and realize *why* you must proceed cautiously. The familiar phrase *caveat emptor,* let the buyer beware, has always applied to the antiques marketplace. Here, then, is a rundown of a few of the most commonly encountered alterations and enhancements you will meet on your search for the great American period piece.

ALTERATIONS AND ENHANCEMENTS

ALTERATIONS

The importance of proportion and scale was discussed in chapter 4. A commonly encountered alteration occurs when a cabinetmaker takes an oversized case piece—a chest of drawers, for example—and cuts it down to a more desirable size. Such alteration can usually be detected by closely scrutinizing the interior joints and construction of the piece. To make a chest of drawers narrower, the drawer fronts need to be reduced. This means that the dovetails will either be recut—fresh cut marks will be the clue here—or eliminated—a lap joint will be used in this case. In addition to this evidence, examination of the case joints, in particular along the edges of the backboards, will reveal areas of fresh saw marks. Or, if the cabinetmaker attempts to conceal his fresh marks, the presence of stain or paint in this unlikely place will be evidence of questionable activity.

ENHANCEMENT

The possibilities for enhancing a piece of furniture are limited only by the imagination of the faker. A piece is said to be enhanced when inlay, carving, and scalloping are used to embellish an originally plain design. The "marrying" of two separate pieces into one piece is also considered a form of enhancement.

Most fakers enhance a piece by adding decoration appropriate to the style and period of the piece. For example, the addition of a carved shell to the center drawer of a case piece or to the knees of table or chair legs in Chippendale furniture is totally appropriate (if somewhat dishonest). In fact, these very embellishments have made more than one unscrupulous dealer wealthy at the expense of the unknowing collector. But few knowledgeable collectors would be fooled if inlay, a decoration used in the later, Hepplewhite period, were added in place of the carving. Yet some fakers know that

uneducated buyers will not detect the incompatability of these mix-matched styles. This is why all collectors must know the decorative motifs appropriate to each period.

Enhancement through recarving can be extremely difficult to detect. And just in case you passed lightly over chapter 10, on patina, you must know that recarving is most easily spotted by comparing the patina of the carved area to the patina of

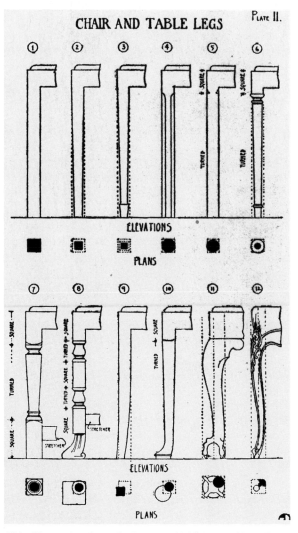

This illustration from the January 1916 issue of Fine Furniture gives the layman a concept of how legs can be recarved or reshaped by the craftsman.

the surrounding area. Old carvings tend to build up residual finish and wax in the crevices and the once-sharp edges of carved surfaces tend to wear down over the decades and centuries. Those raised, carved areas that project beyond the surrounding surfaces are particularly prone to knocks and dents, especially carved chair knees and table legs. The same amount of, if not more, wear should be immediately noticeable on raised, projecting carved areas than is present on the recessed, undecorated surrounding surfaces. Pay special attention to the small dents, nicks, and scratches to the surrounding surface and make sure they continue across the carved surface as well. And of course, be leery of overrefinished pieces where all patina has been removed.

Hepplewhite and Sheraton pieces are frequently enhanced by the addition of inlay, usually decorative bellflower or figural inlays. Few fakers take the time to add a simple checkerboard or geometric inlay. You want to check all elaborate decorative inlay much as you would carving. Scrutinize all surface conditions. Note whether scratches cross the inlaid areas or are deflected due to the ever so slightly raised edge of a newer inlay. A scratch on both sides of an inlaid motif but not across the inlay itself is a sure sign the inlay was added after the scratch. Furthermore, as wood shrinks, small cracks develop at the case joints. Any inlay that crosses these joints will either buckle or break at some point in reaction to the stress caused by the shrinkage. Knowing this, you should be leery of any inlaid piece that has been harshly refinished and had all signs of old patina removed.

One of the easiest forms of enhancement is scalloping, whether of a plain table skirt, top, or leaves; cupboard cornice; cupboard shelves; or apron on a lowboy—to mention only a few possibilities available to the enhancer. This practice frequently occurs on plain country pieces. Luckily, scalloping or the reshaping of these surfaces usually reveals itself in two ways.

First, as insects attack a piece of furniture they produce a small entrance hole connected with vast mazes of small tunnels. Almost all rural furniture has some degree of bug activity, with the exception of cherry, which is almost impervious to insects. When a skirt is scalloped, these tunnels are revealed rather than the small, pin-size entrance holes that will show up on undisturbed surfaces.

Second, when an old surface is reshaped, fresh unpatinated areas become obvious as a result of the new cutting.

When the faker is faced with insect tunnels and unpatinated wood, he will generally try to hide these telltale signs with stain or a thick layer of paint. If you will remember that the edge of a scalloped skirt, cornice, or other surface should reveal an even patina if it is original to the design of the piece, then when you see a heavily, usually irregularly stained or overpainted area, you will be immediately suspicious.

Yet another type of enhancement occurs when the parts of two case pieces, such as highboys, chest on chests, desks, or bookcases, are brought together to form one piece, commonly called a marriage. These unions occur when a dealer, or picker, or faker finds the top to, say, a highboy in one place, and then finds the base to another highboy somewhere else. Once one case has been altered to fit the other, a rather believable highboy has been created out of two separate pieces that were made at different times and never meant for each other.

Such marriages can be detected by first examining the back, not the front, of the piece. (Most people taking the time to create a marriage will be sure the front appears uniform and correct.) Looking at the back, remember that a two-piece case piece, in constant association, will develop an even, continuous patina on the backboards of both cases. If the patina is different on one of the pieces you have evidence this is a marriage. Furthermore, if the backboards of one or both cases have been refinished, stained, or painted this should suggest an attempt to disguise a marriage.

Next look at the fit of the upper and lower cases. There is usually a half-inch step back where the upper case fits onto the bottom case. This means that the upper case is usually a half inch shallower at the front and sides than the bottom case with some form of molding attached to hide this juncture. That narrow molding can be attached to either the upper or lower case. If the step back is either greater or less than a half inch, be suspicious until you are satisfied that the top and bottom did begin life together some two hundred years ago. There are two exceptions to the half-inch rule. One is Queen Anne pieces, which frequently have a step back as great as two inches. The other exception is Pennsylvania Dutch pieces that follow the Germanic tradition of having an upper case that may project as much as two inches beyond the back of the lower case to allow for a flat fit against a wall having a projecting chair rail.

Another way to detect a marriage in those case pieces that have drawers in both sections—chest on chests and highboys—is to carefully examine the drawer construction and dovetailing. The same joinery techniques and similarly sized and shaped dovetails should be present in both cases. This is the test most books on authenticating antiques dwell upon when discussing marriages. And indeed there were many, many marriages created in the late nineteenth and early twentieth centuries by cabinetmakers and dealers.

Ultimately, however, just as with carved and inlaid enhancements, we suggest that marriages should be determined primarily on the basis of patina. When all other signs appear "right" but the patina is "wrong," or there is evidence that the patina has been tampered with or attempts have been made to disguise it, go back and reexamine the piece section by section, point by point.

TRICKS OF THE DECEIVER'S TRADE

Just remember:

- any straight board can be reshaped or recarved
- cabriole knees are often recarved with shell, bellflower, or acanthus-leaf carving

- straight Chippendale chair legs are easily recarved into fret-carved or molded legs
- arms can be added to side chairs
- the frame of upholstered pieces can be easily altered and immediately covered over
- drawers can be added to the aprons of tables, especially Pembroke, tavern, and console tables
- inlay can be added
- drop leaves can be reshaped
- chests, bookcases, sideboards, and other case pieces are easily cut down
- eighteenth-century fall-front desks are sometimes cut-down and converted Empire chests
- straight-leg tables can be made into more stylish splay-leg tables
- large Empire bedposts were easily and often cut down and carved, usually into desirable "rice-carved" beds
- tops or cornices of case pieces are easily added, reshaped, and pierced to suit the current fashion
- tripod pedestal bases of any form, from a candlestand to fire screens, can be reused to make any other pedestal form by adding a new top
- during the first half of the twentieth century, a common practice was to take a period antique and make it into two pieces, each being made up of half old parts and half new parts

This chapter has been designed as a review of the information presented so far. Use it, together with your other reading and your hands-on examination of any furniture said to be antique, as a refresher course now and before you buy.

PART TWO

12

A NOTE TO BEGINNING COLLECTORS

Over the years we have dealt with many collectors whose first purchases were modest but who now have important and valuable collections of American period furniture. The biggest regret all "collectors" who grow into "connoisseurs" have is that they bought too hastily when they were first buying. Most will confess that they were looking for "good deals" and less-expensive items when making those early purchases. Now they all wish they had acquired just one important piece in excellent condition each year rather than the five or ten lesser-quality pieces, often in only acceptable condition, that they bought in haste.

Based on the experiences of others, we suggest that the beginning collector follow three steps before buying the first piece, or, if you have already made some purchases, before you buy the next piece.

First, determine what items you need.

Second, arrange those items in order of your priorities based on the assumption that you will buy only one item each year.

Third, resolve to put the same time and research into each acquisition that you would into purchasing a new house or car.

For example, if you decide a new chest of drawers is your number-one priority for this year, begin by reviewing the marketplace to determine how much you will have to spend to buy that period chest of drawers in the best condition possible that fits within your budget. Having decided that you can spend $5,000, your research will reveal:

1. You can purchase a nice but undistinguished, simple Chippendale chest of drawers with original brasses and finish, or

2. a more impressive Chippendale chest with quarter columns at the side, though, in your price range, the piece will have a fair amount of restoration, as well as replaced brasses, and its ogee feet will be replacements, or

3. you can go for a much finer quality Sheraton chest with original finish and brasses, fluted quarter columns and turned feet, or

4. you can save until you have $10,000 and be able to buy a more impressive Chippendale chest with quarter columns; old, possibly original finish; and original ogee feet.

Once you have assembled this information you can now define your ultimate purpose of why you wish to buy the chest of drawers. Do you want to

furnish your house?
achieve a certain decorative look?
build a collection?
select choice investment pieces?

If you're primarily interested in furnishing your house, your choice can be either 1 or 2, depending on which chest you prefer. If you're trying to achieve a decorative look similar to that most often seen in today's slick-cover life-style magazines, your choice will most likely be 2. A word of warning, however. Because Chippendale chests with quarter columns, even heavily restored, and with replaced feet (an unacceptable state for the connoisseur) are in such demand, those sold by interior-design shops or antiques stores that handle mostly old reproductions or look-alikes rather than period antiques may be overpriced. If you're seeking this sort of piece, rather than the pure period antique, you'll make your best buy at an auction of true period antiques. Connoisseurs will pass the restored chest by, leaving it for you to pick up at a "wholesale" price.

Should your primary interest be in building a collection, you would select 1, 3, or 4, according to your individual taste, pocketbook, and eagerness to make the purchase. And finally, should you decide that a choice investment is your main objective, you would definitely select option number 4. However, the very best collections are owned by those who *love* American antiques, whose purchases are motivated by a desire to *have* these pieces, and for whom the investment factor is a secondary consideration. Often the person solely interested in investment potential will hire an outside adviser rather than developing his own taste and elevating his own knowledge. That person is missing the fun and ultimate rewards of collecting.

LEARNING THE MARKETPLACE

"But," we are often asked, "*where* can we 'learn' the marketplace?"

There are no better barometers of the climate of the market than the international auction houses Sotheby's and Christie's, both with galleries in New York City. There is no substitute for the hands-on examination of the items displayed by these houses before each auction, especially when you have the auction catalog to guide you in your inspection. A few days before each auction you can walk into the gallery, purchase a catalog (if you choose), or use the reference copy provided on the premises, and inspect each piece of furniture by taking the drawers out, turning the piece over or around, and looking and feeling to your heart's content.

However, for those unable to visit New York, careful, continuous study of these auction houses' catalogs and postauction-sale price lists will tell you

- *what* is available in a major segment of the marketplace
- the *condition* of those items offered for sale as noted in the description of each piece
- the *frequency* with which specific pieces come onto the auction floor
- the *comparative* characteristics of similar pieces
- and the *sale price* for each piece at the auction

Over time you will observe the cost of similar pieces of comparable size, quality, materials, style, design, age, rarity, and condition. You will soon learn that most forms—New England Hepplewhite cherry candlestands or Pennsylvania Chippendale quarter-column walnut chests of drawers, for example—will fall into "price bands." Of course, the exceptional piece, whether exceptionally good or exceptionally bad, will always stand apart. But if you seriously "track" like pieces through several auctions you will soon be able to predict sale prices *before* looking at the preauction estimates. When you have reached this stage, you're ready to enter the market with confidence. Remember too that local and regional auction and estate sales will teach you much about pieces and prices in your area.

13

Using the Case Studies

WHAT TO TAKE WITH YOU

Many books and articles written about authenticating period furniture devote much space to listing and explaining the tools you must carry with you and use during your analysis. We recommend that you leave your toolbox at home and take instead your eyes, your hands, and, most important, your common sense and intelligence. Let's face it. You can measure tabletops and take wood samples to your heart's content, but if your mind is closed you'll move right past obvious clues while you're busy trying to impress the world with your technological expertise.

For starters, do whatever you have to do to get the piece you're examining into sufficient light. You simply cannot see the evidence of tool marks and patina when fumbling around in the dark. After that:

Look
Think
Look again
Be skeptical
Then use tools if you need them

TEST YOUR COMMON SENSE

Take a moment to study this purported "eighteenth-century American chair."

To the experienced antiquer its origin isn't even relevant; its date of absolutely no consequence. Why?

107

Your eyes and your common sense should immediately tell you this chair is a *fake!*

How did you come to this conclusion without the aid of anything but your powers of observation?

Look at the worn stretcher. Is there any way it could have been worn down by natural causes? You'd have to be a contortionist to extend your legs back to reach the stretcher while seated in a normal position in this chair! Yet, we can hear someone, somewhere trying to sell this chair, saying, "Just look at the worn stretcher. What wonderful evidence of age!"

HOW KNOWLEDGE OF FORM AND RARITY HELPS

Another example of using common sense and your eyes, combined with your "book knowledge," involves a kettle stand that was stated to be an American eighteenth-century piece. If you take the time to read the many excellent books about the history of American antiques you will learn that kettle stands are rare American forms. And if you take the opportunity to examine furniture carefully, you will quickly observe that even the English "antique" kettle stands are more often made-up pieces than period ones. But even if you haven't reached that stage yet, let's see how common sense held the clue to

learning the truth about a kettle stand I was asked to authenticate and appraise.

This kettle stand had a highly desirable open fret gallery on all four sides and was banded beneath the gallery with a fine beaded border—but on three sides only. A close inspection showed that the beaded border never had been on the fourth side, the very side where the guest would sit when being served tea. The immediate question was, "Why, when the purpose of a kettle stand is to impress your guest, would a fine decorative motif be omitted from the guest's side?" The answer, of course, is, "It wouldn't be." Closer inspection showed the piece to be just like hundreds of other kettle stands—made up.

YOUR FIRST CASE

Let's begin with our first case study of two Queen Anne chairs in the Winterthur collection and see how the eye and a suspicious mind-set helped separate the period chair from the later, nineteenth-century copy. As you walk through this study you will be learning the techniques you must employ each time you set about to answer the question Is it or isn't it?

I observed upon first glance that each of the two chairs, viewed separately and from a distance, looked fine. But the first lesson *you* must learn is that whenever you are looking at a pair, a set, or a group of like pieces, line them up next to each other for close comparison.

When I placed the chairs next to each other two discrepancies immediately jumped out—the difference in the shell carving at the crest rail and the width of the vase-shaped back splat. Yet the crest rail height was almost the same. The thought that first flashed through my mind was that the back splat and shell of one chair would probably prove to be replacements.

But standing back and observing the chairs side by side, once my eyes moved down the length of the chairs two other discrepancies were noted. First there was a difference in seat height between the two chairs. And second, the full knee-width open-

Chair B

Chair A

ing, the distance from the outside of one front knee across to the outside of the other front knee differed between the two chairs. *Four* easily visible differences in dimensions clearly suggested that more was wrong than just the replacing of a back splat. At this point, the tape measure came out for definitive proof because, after all, these were museum property. But note—already the eyes had sufficient proof that the chairs could not be an identical pair.

The differences observed by measuring the chairs were:

	CHAIR A	CHAIR B
Crest height:	$38\frac{3}{8}''$	$38\frac{3}{4}''$
Seat height:	$16\frac{1}{2}''$	$15\frac{3}{4}''$
Back-splat width:	$7\frac{3}{4}''$	$8\frac{3}{4}''$
Knee-width:	$21\frac{1}{4}''$	$21\frac{3}{4}''$
Crest-shell width:	$4''$	$3\frac{1}{2}''$

While taking these measurements and writing them down for comparison, my eye caught another difference on one chair that would help me zero in on which was the "wrong" chair. Look carefully at the left stile on Chair B at the base, where the outward curve ends. Now observe on the same Chair B where the bend on the right stile occurs. There is five-eighths of an inch difference, and once you see it, that discrepancy becomes bigger than life. No eighteenth-century chair *of this quality* and *in its original condition* would have such a discrepancy.

At this point other details began to appear, similar to the details you will find spelled out for you in the illustrated analysis in Case Study 1. These led to the conclusion that Chair A was made in the eighteenth century, and with the exception of a few old repairs, Chair A can be stated to be a c. 1730–1750 carved-mahogany New York State Queen Anne side chair with a value in the $125,000 range. Chair B, on the other hand, though "antique," is out of the period, and its value to the connoisseur is around $2,500.

One last point. As we write this observation, and as you read the analysis, the impression is that this conclusion was reached in just a few minutes. In

reality, by the time the chairs had been looked at, separately at first, then put together, analyzed, measured, carefully examined for repairs, construction, tool marks, quality of carving, patina, and the other fine points we have discussed in Part One, over an hour had flown by. Time is essential to the careful analysis of any fine piece of furniture. That is one reason so many out-of-period pieces are in museums and shops and still being faked today. The usual shopper hasn't the time, and the faker knows this.

NEVER, EVER, BE FORCED INTO MAKING AN INSTANT DECISION.

IN-THE-FIELD USE OF THE CASE STUDIES

The rest of this section is devoted to individual case studies of the forms you are most apt to wish to purchase. There will be much repetition of information if you sit down and read through this section all at one time because many points are identical, regardless of the form or the style. For example, if you are analyzing a Queen Anne highboy and a Hepplewhite secretary-bookcase, you will look for the same evidence on the drawers, no matter that one is a different form and seventy-five years older than the other. But it is essential that we repeat these points so you will have them immediately at hand when you need them in the field.

Next, when you are using this book in the field do not stop with our case study of the form you are analyzing. Check the other pieces from the same period for information that may prove relevant to decorative motifs. For example, if you are considering buying an inlaid Hepplewhite secretary-bookcase, you will not find one in our case studies. But you will find a Chippendale secretary-bookcase. First, follow all the points cited in that case study. Then, review the other Hepplewhite forms that have inlay—the sideboard case study, for example. The combination of these two case studies will guide you in your analysis of the form as well as the style.

THE TREASURE HUNT FOR THE GREAT AMERICAN PERIOD PIECE NEVER ENDS

The search for proof-positive clues to identify fine American period furniture continues from one generation to the next. Countless pages, even books, on this subject have been written over the years. Many authors repeat the same ideas, carry out the same research and analysis, and reach the same conclusions. Only the form and writing styles vary. Yet the audience for the information continues to grow and seek new information and truths. That is why there will always be room for more and more literature on this vast subject. Even as we write these pages, we know that someone probably is beginning to write yet another book or article on "authenticating, identifying, and distinguishing American period furniture, its fakes and reproductions." And why not? Even now fakers are busily attempting to defy our aim and to create fine pieces that will go undetected even by us.

We have been told that in the 1920s and early 1930s, fakers counted it a measure of success when their pieces were deemed "authentic" by noted scholars of the day in books on fine American period antiques.

Next year new books and new fakes will appear simultaneously. Such are the challenges of the antiques marketplace. Don't let this discourage you. Just be sure you're the one who makes the finds. They're being passed by every day.

QUEEN ANNE SIDE CHAIR
(Use for side chairs from all periods.)

STRUCTURAL RESTORATION

Acceptable restoration includes the reinforcement or placement of small patches to the
- crest rail
- splat
- shoe
- frame
- legs
- feet

Acceptable replacements
- one stretcher
- slip-seat frame

WARNING

Visible patches and unsightly repairs to three or more of the areas mentioned, or the patching of both front feet, or replacement of all stretchers can add up to major restoration.

Major restoration includes alteration or enhancement of any portion of the chair through
- recarving of the crest rail, splat, apron, legs, feet
- reshaping of the crest rail, splat, seat frame, apron, legs, feet
- additions, most commonly shell carvings at crest, knees, or apron

Major replacements
- crest rail
- splat
- seat frame—any element—side rails or apron
- leg or legs
- all knee blocks
- full stretcher
- any foot or feet

Major repairs
- major or extensive patches to the splat
- extensive patches or splicing to the front feet or legs

FINISH RESTORATION

Acceptable restoration
replacement or removal of later finishes, leaving as much of original patina as possible

Unacceptable restoration
harsh sanding resulting in a major loss of patina and/or diminishing of aesthetic details (beading, sharpness of carving, crispness of edges)

Although harsh refinishing is not comparable to major structural restoration, it frequently results in substantial value loss.

CHECKPOINTS

1—Crest Rail
Look for mortise and tenon; beware round dowels.

Look carefully at the carving, if present, as it may have been added or enhanced.

2—Splat
Almost always one piece and usually with some beveling or chamfering at the edges of the back of the splat.

Check veneered splats carefully.

3—Shoe
Most will have a two-piece shoe, but there are many exceptions.

Look for nails or glues that are proper.

Screws almost always indicate a repair or re-production.

4—Seat Frame
Look for mortise and tenon; beware round dowels.

Look especially for hand-tool marks or, con-versely, machine-tool marks.

At the front or apron, if a shell is present, check carefully that it is of the period and matches in wear and patina other shells present at the crest rail or knees.

5—Legs
Virtually all period chair legs are carved from one solid piece of wood.

Careful analysis of shell, acanthus, or bellflower carving is essential.

6—Stretchers
At the side, mortised into the legs.

At the median, either mortised or dovetailed into the side stretchers.

Check carefully for false signs of wear or the absence of wear. Compare color, patina, and quality of wood.

7—Feet
Check carefully for replacement and splicing.

Check bottoms for clear indication of centuries of wear.

Check the following for indications of repro-ductions or repairs:

Machine-made dowels: 1. 4. 6.

Screws: 3.

Machine marks: 4. 7.

Fine points:
Pay special attention in chairs to the seats. Note especially the interior blocks at the seat frames and, where present, the slip seats.

Interior blocks at the seat frames: If present, most blocks in period chairs will be glued or attached by period screws or nails. However, modern screws or nails can be added to period chairs to strengthen the frame. If the blocks are original they will match the patina of the inside seat rail. Original blocking is very helpful in determining origin as it is frequently the only secondary wood present for testing except the upholstered seat frame.

Slip-seat frames: Most original slip-seat frames can be identified by

1. indications of numerous layers of up-holstery changes
2. mortise and tenon construction
3. period screws, nails, glue

113

FEDERAL ARMCHAIR
(Use for all armchairs.)

STRUCTURAL RESTORATION

Acceptable restoration includes the reinforcement or placement of small patches to the

crest rail
splat
shield-back surround
arms
frame
legs
stretchers
feet

Acceptable replacements

one stretcher
slip-seat frame

WARNING

Numerous visible patches and unsightly repairs to and extensively broken joints, or the patching of both front feet, or replacement of all stretchers can add up to major restoration.

Major restoration includes alteration or enhancement of any portion of the chair through

recarving of the crest rail, splat, legs or arms
reshaping or enhancement of the inlay, most often at the crest rail, surround, splat, and legs
additional inlay or carving to the crest, surround, splat, apron, legs apron

Major replacements

crest rail
surround
splat
seat frame—any element—side rails or apron
any leg or legs
arms
full stretcher
any foot or feet

Major repairs

major or extensive patches to the shield back, surround, splat, arms, or legs
splicing to the front legs or feet

FINISH RESTORATION

Acceptable restoration

replacement or removal of later finishes, leaving as much of original patina as possible

Unacceptable restoration

harsh sanding resulting in a major loss of patina and/or diminishing of aesthetic details (beading, sharpness of carving, crispness of edges)

Although harsh refinishing is not comparable to major structural restoration, it frequently results in substantial value loss.

CHECKPOINTS

1—Crest Rail and/or Shield Surround

Look for mortise and tenon; beware round dowels.

Check carefully for different color of wood to indicate partial replacements.

2—Splat

Almost always one piece, therefore check carefully for different color of wood to indicate partial replacement, or even full replacement. Replaced splats are frequently two pieces or laminated.

3—Arms

Look for mortise and tenon or peg; beware round dowel.

Arms are frequently added to side chairs, so again check color and wood quality.

Arms are almost always attached by later screws. Wood shrinkage and wear (weight) often cause arms to break. Check to make sure all screw holes match up if there is more than one set present. Screw holes in the seat rail that do not correspond to screw holes in the arms indicate replaced arms. The original screw holes are usually on the inside.

Arms should mortise-and-tenon into the stile.

Look especially for hand-tool marks or, conversely, machine-tool marks.

4—Legs

Period chair legs are carved from one solid piece of wood, especially in the Federal period.

5—Stretchers

At the side, mortised into the legs.

At the median or juncture, either mortised through or dovetailed into the side stretchers.

The stretcher should be flush with the outside of the back legs; usually, but not always, flush with the front legs.

6—Feet

Check carefully for replacement and splicing.

Check bottoms of feet for clear indication of centuries of wear.

Presence of machine marks on the bottoms of the feet indicates either new chair, spliced or tipped legs, or replacement.

Check the following for indications of reproductions or repairs:

Machine-made dowels: 1. 2. 5.

Machine marks: 4. 6.

Fine points:

The original interior glue blocks at the corners of the seat frames will either be glued in or glued in and reinforced with period screws or nails. Because modern screws or nails are often inserted as reinforcements, do not let the presence of later screws or nails color your judgment without careful inspection of the rest of the chair. Original blocks will share a continuity of patina.

Slip-seat frames are *not* a major restoration or repair, but when present, the original seat frame can add to the chair's desirability. Most original slip-seat frames can be identified by

1. indications of numerous layers of upholstery changes
2. mortise and tenon construction
3. period screws, nails, glue

And remember, armchairs are usually slightly wider than side chairs.

CHIPPENDALE CAMELBACK SOFA
(Use for all upholstered pieces.)

Special note. When inspecting upholstered furniture, all or a healthy portion of the upholstery will need to be stripped off for careful analysis of the frame. No truly conclusive analysis of upholstered furniture can be made without such study. Frequently the back and side upholstery panels and the dustcover underneath the bottom can be removed to reveal sufficient area for study.

STRUCTURAL RESTORATION

Acceptable restoration includes

reinforcement or placement of bracing within the frame

small patches to the

frame and leg structure

exposed wood

Acceptable replacement

one or two stretchers

WARNING

Extensive patching and repaired breaks to a number of the legs and stretchers can add up to major restoration.

Major restoration includes

reshaping of the crest rail (often from a straight back into a serpentine or camelback shape) and the arms

recarving or enhancement of the legs and stretchers—beware both blind and open fretwork or elaborate inlay on later sofas

Major replacements

crest rail

arms

major frame elements—upright stiles, front seat frame, etc.

leg or legs

full stretcher

Major repairs

major or extensive patches to the front legs and the majority of the stretchers (though stretcher repair is more acceptable on sofas than on chairs)

splicing to the legs (note that more so on sofas than chairs; sofas often had a full complement of casters that would have been added at a later time—often with the additional removal of 1½ to 2 inches of the original leg—and then, when these casters were removed, to bring the sofa up to proper height, the legs would have been tipped out)

FINISH RESTORATION

Acceptable restoration

replacement or removal of original finish, leaving as much of original patina as possible

Unacceptable restoration

harsh sanding resulting in a major loss of patina and/or diminishing of aesthetic details (beading, sharpness of carving, crispness of edges)

Because pre-1800 period sofas are relatively rare forms, more extensive refinishing and restoration is acceptable, even to the sophisticated collector. Further, the chances are very great that when any sofa is reupholstered, whether for the first, second, or tenth or more time in its two-hundred-year life, it will also have been refinished. For these reasons, refinishing does not diminish the value of a sofa as substantially as it does almost every other form.

CHECKPOINTS

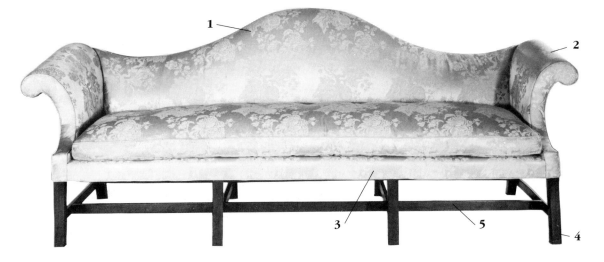

1—Crest Rail

With the upholstery removed, look for mortise and tenon; beware round dowels.

Look carefully for the presence of old and new parts (remember to check for tool marks, nails, screws, and staining—yes, even in the interior) indicating reshaping.

2—Arms

Continue to look for the same points on the arms that you did when examining the crest rail.

Look carefully for the presence of old and new parts, or evidence of a mismatched number of upholstery tacks here from other parts of the frame, indicating new or reshaped arms. Remember, if the sofa happens to have been reupholstered, say, six times, and you find six sets of holes on the frame, you *must* also find six sets of holes on the crest and the arms. This is one way to check for addition of new parts or new shaping.

3—Seat Frame

Look for mortise and tenon; beware round dowels.

Look here especially for hand-tool marks or, conversely, machine-tool marks.

Be sure there is evidence of numerous reupholsterings; in fact, once you're at this point use it as a reference to be sure that all the other elements (crest rail; arms; and the sides, back, and front of the seat frame) show evidence of essentially the same number of reupholsterings.

Expect to find period screws and nails on the frame of a true, authentic period sofa.

Check *inside* (the underneath part) for tool marks, new screws or nails that might indicate the frame has been cut down to a smaller, more desirable size and reattached to the old legs and arms, and possibly even crest rail if the depth has been reduced.

You will need to carefully scrutinize the secondary wood. The majority of period sofas are English, not American, and so the analysis to uncover American woods is essential.

4—Legs

Check bottoms for clear indication of centuries of wear.

Examine carefully to make sure the legs have not been spliced (remember the warning about earlier casters) or even completely replaced. Frequently an early sofa with spliced legs will have had all the legs removed and new ones added.

5—Stretchers

At the side, they should be mortised into the legs; beware round dowels.

Be sure there is no evidence that the stretchers have been moved from an earlier position.

Where the various stretcher parts join each other mortises or dovetailing should be present.

Check carefully for false signs of wear or the absence of wear among the different parts—compare color, patina, and quality of wood—

but remember, more leeway is acceptable here than on chair stretchers. However, if a part or parts are found to have false wear, you should be extremely suspicious about the authenticity of the entire piece. Because sofas are so rare, they present a prime form for the faker.

Many fine sofas will not have stretchers, so while checking in this vicinity, inspect the legs to be sure that stretchers have not been removed.

Check the following for indications of reproductions or repairs:

Machine-made dowels: 1. 2. 3. 5.

Modern screws and nails: 1. 2. 3.

Machine marks: 1. 2. 3. 4. 5.

Fine points:

The frame is of utmost importance in upholstered pieces. There should be ample evidence of hand-tool marks and fasteners on sofa frames. Generally there will be later braces and small patches which, rather than detracting from the value of the period upholstered piece, can be evidence of age, as these were commonly necessary and added when the sofa was reupholstered. Further, the process of reupholstering in itself is the source of abuse to the sofa. The constant reattaching of the fabric and materials in the same general areas of the frame weakens it, often causing it to split or break off. Always remember to look for evidence of the same *number* of sets of upholstery holes on all the elements.

BEDS
(including TESTER BEDS)

STRUCTURAL RESTORATION

Acceptable restoration includes

reinforcement, placement of small patches, or replacement to almost any part, with the exception of unsightly or excessive restoration to the carved posts

Acceptable replacements

tester frame

bed rails

headboard

the lengthening of the legs, though not desirable, is tolerated

> **WARNING**
>
> A large number of visible and unsightly patches or repairs to the footboard, feet, and any carved details can add up to major restoration and extensive devaluation. The replacement of all bed rails plus the headboard is definitely considered major replacement.

Major restoration includes

recarving, reshaping, or enhancement of the posts

extensive tipping of the feet

extensive tipping of the posts

splicing of the end rails, usually associated with a replaced headboard

recarving of the posts

recarving of the feet

Major replacements

removal of the headboard and all rails to substantially enlarge the bed

one or more posts

> **WARNING**
>
> Original headboards are frequently moved to a higher position to accommodate modern mattresses. If two sets of mortise holes exist, check to see if they are the same size. While a repositioned headboard is considered minor, a replaced headboard *in combination with other factors* can be major.
>
> The exception to accepting a replaced headboard would be instances where the headboard is of the tall, paneled type.

Major repairs

extensive rebuilding or patching of posts

extensive rebuilding or patching of the headboard if associated with replaced or heavily altered end rails as well

FINISH RESTORATION

Acceptable restoration

replacement or removal of original finish, leaving as much of original patina as possible

Harsh sanding resulting in a major loss of patina and/or diminishing of aesthetic details (beading, sharpness of carving, crispness of edges) is not as detrimental in beds as in other forms. You can expect the headboard to have been refinished more often than the posts.

CHECKPOINTS

1—Headboard

Does the headboard fit the slots on the posts? Is there indication of even wear and color? If all original elements of the bed are present and the headboard has been replaced, this, *in itself,* is not considered major restoration. Headboards are frequently replaced. If this is the case, evidence in the form of patches or enlarged mortise holes is usually found on the posts.

2—Posts

Check well-carved, small-proportioned posts carefully. We note elsewhere in these pages that large, ungainly bedposts were often re-shaped and carved at a later date. Scrutinize the inside edges of all four posts to see if there are indications of earlier tenon holes for bed rails, headboards, or blanket rails (or even footboards). These are quite frequently present on posts that have been cut down from later, usually Empire, beds, and are now fitted with new parts, and thus the entire bed is, in reality, a made-up slenderized and glamorized piece.

When examining the carving, remember to look for evidence of patina and wear as the giveaway points if the bed has not been heavily refinished.

Spliced or pieced bedposts are another sign of a made-up or heavily restored bed.

3—End Rails

Splicing or replacing of the end rails is considered major because this is usually an indication that the headboard was also replaced when the bed was made wider.

4—Legs and Feet

The legs and posts should be turned from one solid piece of wood. Early beds were never made of laminated wood.

Splicing of the legs is frequently encountered as many beds have been either heightened or shortened and then returned to their original height.

Check the underside of the feet to be sure there is matching wear on all. Fresh tool marks are an indication that the legs have been reduced in height.

Be sure the color of the feet and the posts is the same, as these should be all one piece of wood.

Check the overall proportions of the posts and legs. Short, ungainly legs or posts that do not gracefully taper are an indication that the height has been reduced either from the top or the bottom.

Check the following for indications of reproductions or repairs:

New screws: 1. 2. 3. 4.

Machine marks: 1. 2. 3. 4.

Fine points:

Replacement of the bed rails is generally accepted. However, if the original rails are present, the value is immediately and substantially increased. A totally original bed is most unusual since few survive being taken down and put back up again over the years, as well as moved from one location to another, without the loss or damage to one or more of the many separate parts that make up a bed. At the same time, remember that a bed can be taken apart before you purchase it so all four posts and both side rails can be placed side by side for careful scrutiny and comparison.

CHIPPENDALE CHEST ON CHEST

STRUCTURAL RESTORATION

Acceptable restoration includes
reinforcement, placement of small patches, or minor replacements to the
case
bonnet
drawers
waist molding
feet

Acceptable replacement
up to two or three drawer bottoms
one or even all finials
one back foot and in some cases both back feet

WARNING

A large number of visible and unsightly patches or repairs to the drawers, bonnet, cornice molding, feet, and any carved details can add up to major restoration and extensive devaluation.

Major restoration includes
reshaping of the top
recarving, reshaping, or enhancement of any carved detail
recarving of the feet

Major replacements
bonnet, or major portion of the bonnet molding
any drawer front
any carved detail; for example, at the pilaster
any one front foot and both back feet

Major repairs
extensive rebuilding or patching of drawers
extensive rebuilding or patching of any base molding
extensive rebuilding or patching of the cornice or bonnet

FINISH RESTORATION

Acceptable restoration
replacement or removal of original finish, leaving as much of original patina as possible

Harsh sanding resulting in a major loss of patina and/or diminishing of aesthetic details (beading, sharpness of carving, crispness of edges) is not as detrimental in a large case piece as in other forms because there are many other secondary positions where analysis can determine originality. Though the truly sophisticated connoisseur will always seek an original or truly old finish on even major case pieces, the refinishing and even somewhat harsh sanding of these pieces is deemed acceptable restoration by some collectors.

CHECKPOINTS

1—The Back

Begin here. Check to be sure the top and base match in all points of construction and patina. You're checking to be certain the piece is not a marriage. If needed, refer to chapter 11 under "Enhancements" for a review.

If you find misplaced nail or screw holes, different patinas, stains, paint, improper tool marks, or other indications at the back, question whether the entire piece may be made up. Many large case pieces were created from parts of genuine old pieces during the 1920s antiques-boom era.

Check the piece from the front for proportion. Does the top or base seem too small or large for the piece?

2—Bonnet

Many bonnet tops were once cut down and made into flat tops or flat tops made into bonnet tops. If this occurred there will be a joint running across the face of the bonnet top. Check the closed bonnet for old fasteners. You should find old rosehead nails or sprig nails.

Check the back of the bonnet. You should find the continuity of patina we have spoken of so often.

Look for natural stains and dents and be suspicious of any patterns or unnatural aging marks.

3—Finials

Original finials will add greatly to the value of a chest on chest, but replaced finials are acceptable.

The stem is generally, though not always, part of the old finial, particularly if the finial is of one piece. What you do want to look for are signs of wear and hand-chisel marks.

4—Drawers

Check dovetailing, making sure it matches on all the drawers in both the upper and lower case.

Check the drawer bottoms for evidence of early fasteners.

Check inside the drawers for post holes. More than one set of holes indicates replaced brasses. Refer to chapter 8, the section on brass drawer pulls, for more information on hardware.

Remove the top drawer in both portions of the chest on chest. Now, looking inside, check the top and bottom joints of both cases to make sure they are original and have not been cut down. Frequently tall chest on chests will have one drawer removed from either of the two portions in order to make the height of the chest on chest more suitable to modern houses.

5—Feet

Look closely here. One of the most important proofs of originality in a large case piece is the presence of the original feet at the front. Though it is acceptable to have one and maybe even both of the back feet replaced, the original front feet are of great importance.

Check carefully for splices and major patches.

Check the underside to be sure there are matching tool marks and wear on all of the feet.

Be sure the color of the feet and the base molding is the same, and then compare this with the color of the bottom case. Frequently all feet and the molding have been replaced.

———————

Check the following for indications of reproductions or repairs:

New screws: 1. 2. 4. 5.

Machine marks: 1. 2. 3. 4. 5.

Fine points:

The most common problems encountered with any two-sectional case piece are the replacement or enhancement of the cornice and determining whether the two portions have been married. So begin your inspection by concentrating on these two areas for possible evi-

dence that the piece is not what it is purported to be. The next most likely problem areas are the feet and possibly the base molding. Many ogee bracket feet are later enhancements. If there is a lot of carving on the pieces—blind fret bands, bellflowers, and other similar designs—review chapter 11 on recarving. Any shell carving should be checked carefully as this was a popular enhancement.

On the other hand, the presence of the original finish and brasses on a large case piece like this will double its value. Though acceptable without these original elements, should you happen upon one having original finish and brasses, you've got money in the bank.

HIGHBOYS
(and a few comments on LOWBOYS)

STRUCTURAL RESTORATION

Acceptable restoration includes
reinforcement, placement of small patches, or minor replacement to the
case
bonnet
drawers
waist molding
feet

Acceptable replacement
up to two or three drawer bottoms
one or even all finials
one back foot

WARNING

A large number of visible and unsightly patches or repairs to the drawers, bonnet, cornice molding, feet and any carved details can add up to major restoration and extensive devaluation.

Major restoration includes
reshaping of the top
recarving, reshaping, or enhancement of any carved detail
recarving or reshaping of the apron
recarving of the feet

Major replacements
bonnet, or major portion of the bonnet molding
any drawer front
any carved detail; for example, at the pilaster
any one front foot or more than one back foot

Major repairs
extensive rebuilding or patching of drawers
extensive rebuilding or patching of any base molding

FINISH RESTORATION

Acceptable restoration
replacement or removal of original finish, leaving as much of original patina as possible

Harsh sanding resulting in a major loss of patina and/or diminishing of aesthetic details (beading, sharpness of carving, crispness of edges) is not as detrimental in a large case piece as in other forms because there are many other secondary positions where analysis can determine originality. Though the truly sophisticated connoisseur will always seek an original or truly old finish on even major case pieces, the refinishing and even somewhat harsh sanding of these pieces is deemed acceptable restoration by most collectors.

CHECKPOINTS

1—The Back

Begin here. Check to be sure the top and base match in all points of construction and patina. You're checking to be certain the piece is not a marriage. If needed, refer to chapter 11 under "Enhancements" for a review.

If you find misplaced nail or screw holes, different patinas, stains, paint, improper tool marks, or other indications at the back, question whether the entire piece may be made up. Many large case pieces were created from parts of genuine old pieces during the 1920s antiques-boom era.

Check the piece from the front for proportion. Does the top or base seem too small or large for the piece?

2—Bonnet

Many bonnet tops were once cut down and made into flat tops or flat tops made into bonnet tops. If this occurred there will be a joint running across the face of the bonnet top. Check the closed bonnet for old fasteners. You should find old rosehead nails or sprig nails.

Check the back of the bonnet. You should find the continuity of patina we have spoken of so often.

Look for natural stains and dents and be suspicious of any patterns or unnatural aging marks.

3—Finials and Drops

Original finials and drops will add greatly to the value of a highboy, but replaced finials and drops are acceptable.

The stem is generally, though not always, part of the old finial or drop, particularly if the finial or drop is of one piece. What you do want to look for are signs of wear and hand-chisel marks.

4—Drawers

Check dovetailing, making sure it matches on all the drawers in both the upper and lower case.

Check the drawer bottoms for evidence of early fasteners.

Check inside the drawers for post holes. More than one set of holes indicates replaced

brasses. Refer to chapter 8, the section on brass drawer pulls, for additional information on hardware.

Remove the top drawer in both portions of the highboy. Now, looking inside, check the top and bottom joints of both cases to make sure they are original and have not been cut down. Frequently tall highboys will have one drawer removed from either of the two portions in order to make the height more suitable to modern houses.

5—Skirt or Apron

Check carefully for evidence of reshaping, a frequent enhancement.

Any carving should be scrutinized for originality.

Remember to look for evidence of patina and wear as the giveaway points.

6—Legs

Legs should be one piece going from the foot all the way up through the front stile. The exception to this is that Rhode Island–area pieces will frequently have a detachable leg, with the leg actually mortised into the bottom of the case.

Splicing of the legs may be the most frequently encountered problem in highboys and lowboys, so check carefully.

Check any carving to be sure it is original.

7—Feet

Look closely here. One of the most important points of originality in a large case piece is the presence of the original feet at the front. Though it is acceptable to have one back foot replaced, the original front feet are of great importance.

Check carefully for splices and major patches.

Check the underside to be sure there are matching tool marks and wear on all of the feet.

Be sure the color of the feet and the base molding is the same, and then compare this with the color of the bottom case. Frequently all feet and the molding have been replaced.

Check the following for indications of reproductions or repairs:

New screws: 1. 2. 4. 5. 6. 7.

Machine marks: 1. 2. 3. 4. 5. 6. 7.

Fine points:

The most common problems encountered with any two-sectional case piece are identifying the replacement or enhancement of the cornice and determining whether the two portions have been married. So begin your inspection by concentrating on these two areas for possible evidence that the piece is not what it is purported to be. The next most likely problem areas are the feet and moldings. Many ogee bracket feet are later enhancements. If there is a lot of carving on the pieces—blind fret bands, bellflowers, and other similar designs—review chapter 11 on recarving. Any shell carving should be checked carefully as this was a popular enhancement.

On the other hand, the presence of the original finish and brasses on a large case piece like this will double its value. Though acceptable without these original elements, should you happen upon one with the assets of original finish and brasses, you've got money in the bank.

Lowboys: Although the checkpoints supplied for the case studies of the Pembroke table and chest of drawers cover all the elements of the lowboy, because some highboy bases have been converted into lowboys this information is included here.

Highboy bases found with their tops no longer present have traditionally been turned into "lowboys" because they look like lowboys. In reality, in no manner, form, or shape do highboy bases have the same proportions as lowboys. Any lowboy offered to you that is in excess of twenty-eight inches high is actually the base of a highboy with a new top. Highboy bases will range from twenty-eight to thirty-five inches tall. Lowboys range from twenty-six to twenty-eight inches tall. Of course, there is also the corresponding difference in the width of these two forms.

CHIPPENDALE SECRETARY BOOKCASE
(includes fall-front desks without the bookcase present)

STRUCTURAL RESTORATION

Acceptable restoration includes

reinforcement, placement of small patches, or minor replacement to the

case
cornice
broken arch top (if present)
astragal moldings of glazed doors
interior bookcase shelves
drawers
feet

Acceptable replacements

up to two or three large drawer bottoms
prospect door, acceptable but not desirable
most of the scalloped valances above the cubbyholes
one or two of the small interior drawers
one back foot and in some cases both back feet
the interior bookcase shelves

WARNING

A large number of visible and unsightly patches or repairs to the drawers, top, cornice molding, feet, or the replacement of numerous of the valances and/or small drawers, though not in themselves major, can add up to major restoration and extensive devaluation.

Major restoration includes

reshaping of the top
recarving, reshaping, or enhancement of any carved detail
recarving, reshaping, or enhancement of the interior desk compartment
recarving of the feet
reduction of the case size in any way

Major replacements

broken arch top or major portion of the top molding
transition from glazed doors to solid panel doors or vice versa
replacement of the interior or desk compartment
replacement of the writing slant or fall board
any drawer front
any carved detail; for example, at the pilaster or cornice
any one front foot or both back feet
the lowering or heightening of the case
any marriage

Major repairs

extensive rebuilding or patching of drawers
extensive rebuilding or patching of any base molding
extensive rebuilding or patching of the cornice
extensive rebuilding or patching of the upper case doors

FINISH RESTORATION

Acceptable restoration

replacement or removal of original finish, leaving as much of original patina as possible

Harsh sanding resulting in a major loss of patina and/or diminishing of aesthetic details (beading, sharpness of carving, crispness of edges) may be considered major, and is major on a desk alone. However, secretary bookcases, being double case pieces, are allowed to have more refinishing than single case pieces. See the notes under "acceptable restoration" for the Chippendale chest on chest (Case Study 5). Remember, though, the presence of an original finish can greatly increase the value of a secretary bookcase, as will the presence of original brasses.

ADDITIONAL POINTS

Where the bookcase and desk meet, the molding can be attached to either the top case or the bottom case.

Exposed dovetails on the top of the desk: Desks were frequently made with exposed dovetails, so do not assume that a desk with dovetails showing has "lost" its bookcase top. Generally more sophisticated or urban cabinetmakers used full-blind dovetails at the top, but there are exceptions even to this rule of thumb.

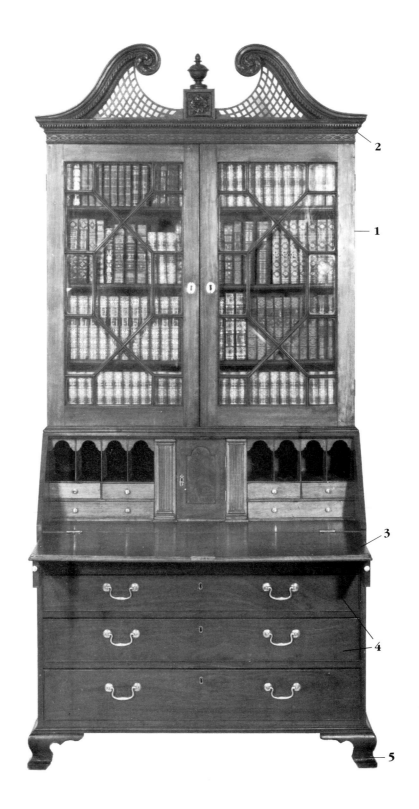

CHECKPOINTS

1—The Back

Begin here and reread the Warning on page 127. Check to be sure the top and base match in all points of construction and patina. You're checking to be certain the piece is not a marriage. If needed, refer to chapter 11 under "Enhancements" for a review.

If you find misplaced screw holes, different patinas, stains, paints, improper tool marks, or other indications at the back, question whether the entire piece may be made up. Many large case pieces were created from old parts during the 1920s antiques-boom era.

Check the piece from the front for proportion. Does the top or base seem too small or large for the piece?

2—Top

Many secretary tops were once cut down, made into flat tops, or flat tops were converted into broken arch tops. If this occurred there will be a joint running across the face of the cornice. Check for old fasteners on closed bonnet tops. You should find old rosehead nails or sprig nails.

Check the back edge of arched or flat molded tops. You should find the continuity of patina we have spoken of so often.

Look for natural stains and dents and be suspicious of any patterns or unnatural aging marks.

3—Fall Board or Writing Slant

It is all right to find fall boards reset and evidence of corresponding old hinge marks or patches. What you do *not* want to find is evidence of old hinge marks on the case and *not* on the fall board itself, or vice versa, as either one would indicate the introduction of a new fall board.

Look for shrinkage along the bread-board banding with the side boards extending as much as a sixteenth or an eighth of an inch beyond the end of the broad desk surface. Frequently there will be a split along the mitered edge as well.

4—Drawers

Check dovetailing, making sure it matches on all the drawers in both the upper and lower case.

Check the drawer bottoms for evidence of early fasteners.

Check the inside of the drawers for post holes for both period screws and later modern screws. If more than one set of holes is evident, the present set is a replacement.

Remove the top drawer in the bottom or desk portion. Now, looking inside, check the interior joints to make sure they are original and have not been cut down. Frequently tall secretaries will have one drawer removed in order to make the height of the chest on chest more suitable to modern houses. Almost all secretaries and desks should have four tiers of drawers. The top drawer tier may have two or, rarely, three drawers over three long drawers. Desks with only three tiers of drawers, unless country pieces, should be examined carefully. Candle slides, though legitimately found, were a popular form of enhancement, so if these are present, check the edges and inside of the case for new tool marks and disturbed patina to be sure all parts appear original.

5—Feet

Look closely here. One of the most important points of originality in a large case piece is the presence of the original feet at the front. Though it is acceptable to have one back foot, and maybe even both back feet, replaced, the original front feet are of great importance.

Check carefully for splices and major patches.

Check the underside to be sure there are matching tool marks and wear on all of the feet.

Be sure the color of the feet and the base molding is the same, and then compare this with the color of the bottom case. Frequently all feet and the molding have been replaced.

Check the following for indications of reproductions or repairs:

New screws: 1. 2. 4. 5.

Machine marks: 1. 2. 3. 4. 5.

Fine points:

The most common problems encountered with any two-sectional case piece are identifying replacement or enhancement of the cornice and determining whether the two sections have been married. We have emphasized that secretary bookcases are particularly prone to marriages, if for no other reason than that they are such desirable pieces. So begin your inspection by concentrating on these two areas for possible evidence that the piece is not what it is purported to be. The next most likely problem areas are the feet and possibly the base molding. Many ogee bracket feet are later enhancements. If there is a lot of carving on the pieces—blind fret bands, bellflowers, and other similar designs—review chapter 11 on recarving. Any shell carving should be checked carefully as this was a popular enhancement. Also, remember to be particularly wary of secretary bookcases with ornate bonnets or broken arch pediments as well as double-domed bookcase sections with glazed doors.

On the positive side, the presence of the original finish and brasses on a large case piece like this will double its value. Though acceptable without these original elements, should you find one with these assets you are indeed fortunate.

CUPBOARDS

(including corner cupboards, open and doored cupboards, hanging shelves, and similar forms)

Special note: Period cupboards, unlike period secretary bookcases, chests on chests, and highboys, can be found in both one- and two-part construction. It goes without saying that if the cupboard has two cases, be sure to check for a marriage.

STRUCTURAL RESTORATION

Acceptable restoration includes
reinforcement, placement of small patches, or minor replacements to the
case
cornice
broken arch top (if present)
interior cupboard shelves
waist molding
drawers
doors
feet

Acceptable replacements
up to two or three drawer bottoms in cupboards with drawers
the glass (or panes) in glazed-door pieces
one back foot, sometimes both
one or two of the interior shelves

WARNING

A large number of visible and unsightly patches or repairs to the case, top, cornice molding or feet, though not in themselves major, can add up to major restoration and extensive devaluation.

Major restoration includes
reshaping of the top
recarving, reshaping, or enhancement of any carved detail

recarving, reshaping, or enhancement of the interior shelves
recarving, reshaping, or enhancement of straight sides, usually in the form of scalloping
removal or replacement of doors
recarving of the feet

Major replacements
broken arch top or major portion of the top molding
transition from glazed doors to solid panel doors or vice versa
replacement of all the interior shelves; usually they will be shaped as well as replaced
replacement of any drawer front
replacement of any carved detail; for example, at the pilaster or waist molding
replacement of any one front foot or both back feet
lowering or heightening the case
any marriage

Major repairs
extensive rebuilding or patching of doors, sides, or drawers
extensive rebuilding or patching of any moldings
extensive rebuilding or patching of the feet

FINISH RESTORATION

Acceptable restoration
replacement or removal of original finish, leaving as much of original patina as possible

Harsh sanding resulting in a major loss of patina and/or diminishing of aesthetic details (beading, sharpness of carving, crispness of edges) may be considered major. Extreme refinishing will drastically affect the value, but it will not "kill" the piece, the way it would a candlestand, for example. You should check the notes under "acceptable restoration" for the Chippendale chest on chest (Case Study 5). Remember, though, the presence of an original finish can greatly appreciate the value of a cupboard, as will the presence of original glass if the doors are glazed.

CHECKPOINTS

1—The Back

Begin here and reread the Warning on page 131. If the cupboard is in two parts you're also checking to be certain the piece is not a marriage. Check to be sure the top and base match in all points of construction and patina. If needed, refer to chapter 11 under "Enhancements" for a review.

If you find misplaced screw holes, different patinas, stains, paints, tool marks, or other indications at the back, question whether the entire piece may be made up. Remember our warning (page 131).

Realizing how many cupboards have problems, check the piece from the front for proportion. Ask yourself, Does the top or base seem too small or large for the piece? Is the piece slender and more suited to a modern-size room than to an eighteenth- or nineteenth-century room? If so, might it have been cut down, or simply made up?

2—Top

Many cupboard tops have been enhanced over the years to make these often utilitarian pieces more glamorous. Review the sections relating to new tops under other case pieces and remember to check the top of any scalloped top for paint, stain, or other means to conceal fresh cutting marks.

While examining the top from the back and the front you should find the continuity of patina we have spoken of so often.

Look for natural stains and dents and be suspicious of any patterns or unnatural aging marks.

3—Doors and Openings

The warnings given relating to replacing, restoring, reshaping, and even redesigning of doors and openings on cupboards cannot be overemphasized. Check all surfaces for suspicious hinge, screw, or nail marks, as well as fresh cut or tool marks. When doors are removed, the returns or stiles are frequently scalloped or cut down to remove the old hinge marks. Then shaped shelves are added. Carefully inspect the shelves to be sure there are no nail holes that would indicate the returns have been cut back.

Check the mortise and tenon joints, making sure they match on all the doors in both the upper and lower case.

4—Drawers

Check the dovetailing, making sure it matches on all the drawers in both the upper and lower case.

Check the drawer bottoms for evidence of early fasteners.

Check inside the drawers and review chapter 8 on brasses.

If examining a corner cupboard with a drawer or mixing shelf in the middle portion, remove it and check the sides of this part as well as inside the case to be sure it is not a later addition.

5—Feet

Look closely. Because cupboards receive more wear than many other large case pieces the feet have often been repaired and even replaced. Replaced feet, especially on corner cupboards, are more often tolerated here than they would be on other forms.

Check carefully for splices and major patches.

Check the underside to be sure there are matching tool marks and wear on all of the feet.

Be sure the color of the feet and the base molding is the same, and then compare this with the color of the bottom case. Frequently all feet and the molding have been replaced.

Check the following for indications of reproductions or repairs:

New screws: 1. 2. 3. 4.

Machine marks: 1. 2. 3. 4. 5.

Fine points:

The most common problem with cupboards is that the demand has far exceeded the supply of period pieces over the years. The plainer the cupboard, the greater its chances of being original. Further, because cupboards span such a long period, many eighteenth-century cupboards were enhanced during the nineteenth century to make them appear more contemporary and stylish. Inlay was added, stenciled patterns were applied, and even fancy hardware and new tops and feet were attached to perfectly fine, though plain, unpretentious cupboards in the name of fashion and economy.

On the positive side, cupboards in their original condition, especially those with the original finish and hardware, do exist and are often uncovered in, yes, country auctions and antiques shops. But don't expect them to have "country" prices anymore.

SIDEBOARDS

STRUCTURAL RESTORATION

Acceptable restoration includes

reinforcement or placement of small patches to the

top
drawers or cabinets
case
legs
feet

Acceptable replacements

minor replacement to the inlay, crossbanding, or veneer

replacement of one or two drawer bottoms, cabinet shelves, or some reworking of interior compartments

---

WARNING

Although restoration of the original drawers or compartments—that is, the dividers or shelves inside—in itself is not major restoration, the replacement or removal of a large portion or all these elements can result in major redesigning of the piece, rendering the piece "altered." And of course unsightly or large patches of the top, case, legs, drawers, or apron can add up to major restoration and extensive devaluation.

Major restoration includes

reshaping or altering the top
the addition of inlay or crossbanding
replacement or enhancement of the majority of the inlay
converting a drawer into a cupboard door or vice versa
heightening or extending the legs
recarving, reshaping, or enhancement of the legs and feet
the introduction of (addition of) a drawer

Major replacements

top
any drawer or cupboard face
any one or more of the legs
one or more feet

Major repairs

major or extensive patches to the top, front, sides, or legs
splicing to the legs or feet
extensive repair to the inlay or veneer

FINISH RESTORATION

Acceptable restoration

replacement or removal of original finish, leaving as much of the original patina as possible. Due to the thinness of such a long board, sideboard tops often split. Repairs to the tops, especially in areas where they are not immediately visible (usually when covered by decorative candlesticks or a silver service), are more acceptable on sideboards than on some other pieces.

Unacceptable restoration

harsh sanding resulting in a major loss of patina and/or diminishing of aesthetic details (beading, inlay, sharpness of carving, crispness of edges)

Harsh refinishing of sideboard tops may be tolerated with greater leniency, but it can substantially affect the monetary worth of the piece.

1—Top

Check the underside of the top to make sure it is original. Because so many tops have split over the years, they are frequently replaced. Better to have a split and repaired top than a new one.

Look underneath the top for screw holes, different patinas, stains, paints, tool marks, or other indications that the top may have originally been part of another piece of furniture but was suitable for use as old wood on the sideboard base.

Feel for the rippling of hand planing.

Look for natural stains and dents and be suspicious of any signs of artificial wear and staining.

2—Frame

Frequently a large, ungainly nineteenth-century sideboard is cut down to create a streamlined, more desirable "eighteenth-century-style" sideboard. Careful scrutiny of the inside frame will reveal signs of this alteration: tool marks, modern screws, fasteners, and locks, as well as fresh wood cuts and stained or painted-over areas.

Check for misplaced nail holes, which would indicate that the sideboard (or parts of it) was made up of old wood.

Check inside the drawer opening to be sure there are no tenons or hinge scars visible, which would indicate they had been cut to add a drawer or that a drawer has been added where previously there had been a cupboard door.

Check the back and the bottom for through tenon joints and good patina as evidence of age. On the other hand, paint or stain and modern tool marks or hardware will be warning signs.

3—Drawers and/or Cupboard Doors

Check the dovetailing of drawers.

Check the brasses for proper wear and origi-

nality, and make sure that if there are two or more sets of holes on the inside of the drawer there are corresponding holes on the exterior face of the drawer. If not, the drawer front has been reveneered.

Check cupboard or cabinet doors to make sure these were not originally cellarette drawers. Look closely at the edge of the door. If there is a heavy patch running along each side of the door this will be an indication that the door was originally a drawer and the patches are concealing dovetail slots. On the interior, there will be "shadows," a difference in patina, or evidence that drawer runners were once present. If the change is vice versa, the opening edges will have patched hinge marks.

Hinges on doors are frequently replaced. Patches covering old hinge marks should conform to both the door and the frame. If such marks are not present, a major element has been replaced, usually the door.

4—Inlay

Check all inlay carefully to make sure it has not been added. Pay special attention to the cuff of the legs. Frequently sideboard legs have been extended by adding or tipping the legs. The joint securing this new portion will be inside the cuff. Therefore, check the grain and color of the woods above and beneath the cuff, being sure there is a continuous flow of grain and matching color on both sides of the cuffs on all the legs.

5—Legs and Feet

Be sure the legs are one continuous piece beginning at the top, where they are mortise-and-tenoned into the frame. Many legs have been replaced at the skirt or apron level.

Check carefully for splices and major patches.

Check the underside to be sure there are matching tool marks and wear on all of the legs. Frequently one or more legs will be replaced.

Be sure the color of all the legs is the same. Frequently all legs have been replaced.

Double-check the cuff if the legs have one. Refer back to the inlay detail.

Check the following for indications of reproductions or repair:

New screws and hinges: 1. 2. 3.

Machine marks: 1. 2. 3. 5.

Machine-cut dovetailing: 2. 3.

Fine points:

Check the shape and dimension of the top in relationship to the base. A serpentine base should certainly have a conforming top. Stop and ask yourself, Why would the time and trouble be put into the construction of an elaborate, sophisticated base and a simple, straight-edge top put on it? It is conceivable that the original top is still on the piece and that its curves were cut off at some later time, but if that is so, would you want to pay a premium price?

CHIPPENDALE BIRDCAGE TEA TABLE
(Use for pedestal tables, including candlestands and fire or pole screens.)

STRUCTURAL RESTORATION

Acceptable restoration includes
  reinforcement or placement of small patches to the
  top
  tilt mechanism
  pedestal
  leg juncture
  legs
  feet

Acceptable replacements
  one spindle of the birdcage
  latch
  one batten under the tabletop

W A R N I N G

Unsightly or large patches of the top or pedestal at the leg juncture can add up to major restoration and extensive devaluation, as does an extensive patch to any of the feet or reinforcement patch to a leg (frequently broken on these tables).

Major restoration includes
  reshaping of the tabletop
  adding birdcage mechanism where none previously existed
  recarving, reshaping, or enhancement of the pedestal, legs, and feet

Major replacements
  top
  both battens under the tabletop
  birdcage mechanism
  pedestal
  one or more legs
  one or more feet

Major repairs
  major or extensive patches to the top, pedestal, or legs
  splicing to the legs or feet

FINISH RESTORATION

Acceptable restoration
  replacement or removal of original finish, leaving as much of original patina as possible

Unacceptable restoration
  harsh sanding, resulting in a major loss of patina and/or diminishing of aesthetic details (beading, sharpness of carving, crispness of edges)

Harsh refinishing of tea tables and candlestands is comparable to major restoration. Because these tables and stands are frequently restored and are the most common of the outright fakes, the original patina and/or finish becomes more essential in the total analysis of these forms than in other pieces.

CHECKPOINTS

1—Top

If the top is round, measure it and look for proper shrinkage.

Feel for the rippling of hand planing.

Look for natural stains, dents, and genuine signs of wear.

Look underneath the top for screw holes, different patina, stains, paint, tool marks, or other indications that the top originally may have been part of another piece of furniture but was suitable for cutting down for use of old wood on either an old or new pedestal.

Because tops are frequently replaced or reshaped, check for proportion. Does the top seem too small or ungainly large?

Almost all round tops under eighteen inches are one piece of wood, though we have seen one board top as wide as thirty-two inches. If the top is over eighteen inches, it is perfectly all right for two boards to have been used originally. Do not let a two-board top *alone* convince you that a wide table is not right.

2—Battens

Due to shrinkage, battens need to be moved or reset at some time over the years. If not, the top will split.

Check for both period screws and later modern screws. If modern screws are present, there will most likely be two sets of holes, one for the original set and one for the second set. Be careful to note whether the screw holes in the battens match the holes in the top.

3—Birdcage tilt mechanism

There should be matching dents and areas of wear on the top of the mechanism and the bottom of the tabletop where the two are in contact. There should be wear on the sleeve and turning mechanism itself, indicating the spinning of the tabletop.

Birdcage mechanisms are fragile. Check for expected wear and replacements.

4—Pedestal

Check for enhancement if elaborately carved.

5—Leg Juncture

Look for dovetailing where the legs are slotted into the pedestal on the underside.

6—Legs and Feet

Check carefully for splices and major patches.

Check the underside to be sure there are

matching tool marks and wear on all of the legs. Frequently, one or more legs will be replaced.

Be sure the color of the pedestal and all three of the legs is the same, as sometimes all legs have been replaced.

The leg and foot should be one piece. Because the foot, especially if ball and claw carved, is often wider than the leg, lamination lines on the sides are an indication that more wood was added for later carving, reshaping, or enhancement. There are a few exceptions to this rule—primarily Philadelphia and New York tables having exceptionally wide ball-and-claw feet.

———————————

Check the following for indications of reproductions or repairs:

Machine-made dowels: 5.

New screws: 1. 2.

Machine marks: 1. 2. 5. 6.

Fine points:

Original finish is of tremendous importance. Moving pieces that come in contact with each other should show matching wear. Even on a simple Hepplewhite oval-top candlestand, there should be dents and wear where the tilting mechanism comes in contact with the underneath part of the top of the table—when the top is in a tilted rather than tabletop position. Additional checks can be made on the pedestal if there are round parts to establish proper shrinkage. However, if the table or stand is mahogany, keep in mind that there will not be as much shrinkage as if the piece were walnut, cherry, apple, or maple.

PEMBROKE TABLE
(Use for all drop-leaf pieces.)

STRUCTURAL RESTORATION

Acceptable restoration includes
   reinforcement or placement of small patches to the
   top, especially around the hinges
   legs
   feet

Acceptable replacements
   minor replacement to the inlay and crossbanding
   replacement of the drawer bottom, or new drawer runners
   reset top, with addition of some glue blocks

W A R N I N G

Unsightly or large patches of the top, leaf (or leaves), leg, drawer (or drawers), or apron can add up to major restoration and extensive devaluation.

Major restoration includes
   reshaping or alteration of the tabletop, or the addition of inlay and crossbanding
   reshaping or alteration, usually addition of inlay, of the leaf or leaves
   replacement or enhancement of the majority of the inlay
   heightening or extending of the skirt, legs, or feet
   recarving, reshaping, or enhancement of the legs and feet
   the introduction of (addition of) a drawer

Major replacements
   top
   one or both leaves
   drawer
   one or more of the legs

   the swing-gate mechanism of the drop leaf or leaves
   splicing of one or more feet

Major repairs
   major or extensive patches to the top, leaf or leaves, or legs
   splicing to the legs or feet
   extensive repair to the inlay

FINISH RESTORATION

Acceptable restoration
   replacement or removal of original finish, leaving as much of the original patina as possible

Unacceptable restoration
   harsh sanding resulting in a major loss of patina and/or diminishing of aesthetic details (beading, sharpness of carving, crispness of edges)

Harsh refinishing removes evidence in the surface condition important in determining the originality of the parts of drop-leaf tables. Therefore, an extensively sanded, refinished piece will be considerably devalued.

CHECKPOINTS

1—Top

Check the underside of the top to make sure there is evidence of swing-gate wear on the proper place on the leaves.

The presence of new screws is acceptable because when the top shrinks the screws will fall out and be replaced. But there should be ample wear around the screw holes indicating that the holes are older than the screws, or else there will be more than one set of holes. If the old screw holes are present, take a straw and stick it into the hole, making sure it goes into the top where the old screw went through.

Feel for the rippling of hand planing.

Look for natural stains and dents and be suspicious of any patterns or individual aging marks.

Look underneath the top for screw holes, different patinas, stains, paints, tool marks, or

other indications that the top may have originally been part of another piece of furniture but was suitable for cutting down for use as old wood on either an old or new pedestal.

Hinges are frequently replaced. Patches covering old hinge marks should conform to both the leaf and the top. If such marks are not present, a major element has been replaced, usually the leaf.

Because leaves on drop-leaf tables are frequently replaced or reshaped, check for proportion. Does the top seem too small or ungainly large?

2—Frame

Check for proper joints at the corners.

Check for tool marks.

Check inside of the drawer opening to be sure

there are no tenons visible, which would indicate they had been cut to add a drawer.

Check for misplaced nail holes, particularly around the apron and drawer, which would indicate that the table or these parts were made up of old wood.

3—Drawer

Check the dovetailing.

Check the brasses for proper wear and originality. Be sure that if there are two or more sets of holes on the face of the drawer there are corresponding holes on the interior of the drawer. If not, the drawer front is not original.

4—Inlay

It is essential to check all inlay carefully to make sure it has not been added. Pay special attention to the cuff of the legs. Frequently table legs have been extended by adding or tipping the legs. The joint securing this new portion will be inside the cuff. Therefore, check the grain and color of the woods both above and beneath the cuff, being sure there is a continuous flow of grain and matching color on both sides (above and below) of the cuffs on all the legs.

5—Legs and Feet
Check carefully for splices and major patches.

Check the underside to be sure there are matching tool marks and wear on all of the legs. Frequently one or more legs have been replaced.

Be sure the color of all the legs is the same, as sometimes all legs have been replaced.

Check the following for indications of reproductions or repairs:

New screws and hinges: 1. 2.

Machine marks: 1. 2. 3. 5.

Dovetailing: 2.

Fine points:
Plain Pembroke tables outnumber inlaid Pembroke tables a thousand to one. At the same time, an inlaid Pembroke table is considered by most collectors a thousand times more valuable than a plain Pembroke table. The result? Countless numbers of plain Pembroke tables have been enhanced at some time during their lifetime. These true eighteenth- and early-nineteenth-century tables may be perfectly fine, with the exception of the later, added inlay.

When inlay has been added, it is usually on the grander scale—bellflowers, husks, eagles, or other elaborate designs. Realizing this, you should proceed cautiously. When examining inlay remember that original inlay is usually quite flush to the surrounding wood surface. Replaced inlay often projects slightly above the wood surface. Notice in detail the scratches,

dents, and shrinkage to the frame or surrounding areas. Scratches and dents should be *obvious* in the inlay as well. Where the frame shows evidence of shrinkage there should be breaks in the inlay. Remember, too, inlay is of a different wood from that surrounding it. Therefore, over the years, as both woods continue to breathe, shrink, and swell, inlay no longer secured tightly by the surrounding wood may loosen and pop out, often being lost. So look for small elements of the original inlay to be either missing or to have been replaced. If the piece has been extensively refinished, there can be no way to determine if the inlay has been replaced or added, so be wary of pristine inlaid pieces where the frame appears to have all the marks of the eighteenth or early nineteenth century.

At the same time, remember, too, that a large portion of inlaid Pembroke tables in the marketplace are, in reality, fakes—made up from old parts.

BIBLIOGRAPHY

American Manufactured Furniture. West Chester, Pennsylvania: Schiffer Publishing Ltd., 1988.

Bishop, Robert. *How to Know American Antique Furniture*. New York: E. P. Dutton, 1973.

Bjerkoe, Ethyl Hall. *The Cabinetmakers of America*. Exton, Pennsylvania: Schiffer Publishing Ltd., 1978.

Bly, John, ed. *The Confident Collector*. New York: Prentice-Hall Press, 1986.

Butler, Joseph T. *Field Guide to American Antique Furniture*. New York: Roundtree Press–Facts on File Publications, 1985.

Furniture: As Interpreted by the Century Furniture Company. Grand Rapids, Michigan, 1937.

Cescinsky, Herbert. *The Gentle Art of Faking Furniture*. New York: Dover Publications, 1967.

Comstock, Helen, ed. *The Concise Encyclopedia of American Antiques*. New York: Hawthorn Publishers, Inc., 1984.

Darling, Sharon. *Chicago Furniture: Art, Craft, & Industry, 1833–1983*. New York: W. W. Norton & Company, 1984.

Downs, Joseph. *American Furniture in the Winterthur Museum*. New York: Macmillan Publishing Company, 1952.

————. *American Furniture: Queen Anne and Chippendale Periods*. New York: Bonanza Books, 1952.

Federhen, Deborah A., et al. *Accumulation & Display: Mass Marketing Household Goods in America, 1880–1920*. Winterthur, Delaware: The Henry Francis du Pont Winterthur Museum, 1986.

Fairbanks, L., and Elizabeth B. Bates. *American Furniture: 1620–Present*. New York: Richard Marek Publishers, 1981.

Fales, Dean A., Jr. *American Painted Furniture, 1660–1880*. New York: E. P. Dutton, 1979.

Naeve, Milo M. *Identifying American Furniture: A Pictorial Guide to Styles and Terms, Colonial to Contemporary*. Nashville, Tennessee: The American Association for State and Local History, 1981.

Paxton, Frank. *Beautiful Woods*. Kansas City, Missouri: Frank Paxton Lumber Company, 1974.

Sack, Albert. *Fine Points of American Furniture: Early American*. New York: Crown Publishers, Inc., 1982.

Schiffer, Nancy N. and Herbert F. *Woods We Live With*. West Chester, Pennsylvania: Schiffer Publishing Ltd., 1977.

Smith, Nancy. *Old Furniture: Understanding the Craftsman's Art*. New York: Dover Publications, 1990.

ACKNOWLEDGMENTS

Knowledge is not gained quickly or from one source. Joe and I have learned, individually and collectively, from everyone who loves and values antiques with whom we have come in contact over the years—from dealers to collectors. Thank you for the stories, advice, and information you have shared with us.

Thank you, especially, James Craig and Sam Tarlton of Craig and Tarlton, Inc., Charles Hummel and Nancy Evans of Winterthur, Frank Horton and the staff at the Museum of Early Southern Decorative Arts, the Rhode Island School of Design, Carl Voncannon at the Furniture Library in High Point, North Carolina, Walter Keller, Sam Pennington, Steve Minor, and Bruce Johnson.

And once again, thank you, Susan Urstadt and Ann Cahn, for good advice, friendly dispositions, and the sharing of our vision.

INDEX